THE PRIVILEGES OF BISHOPS

COMMENTARY WITH HISTORICAL NOTES

THE CATHOLIC UNIVERSITY OF AMERICA
CANON LAW STUDIES
No. 282

The Privileges of Bishops

Commentary with Historical Notes

A DISSERTATION

SUBMITTED TO THE FACULTY OF THE SCHOOL OF CANON LAW OF THE CATHOLIC UNIVERSITY OF AMERICA IN PARTIAL FULFILLMENT OF THE REQUIREMENTS FOR THE DEGREE OF DOCTOR OF CANON LAW

BY THE
REV. FRANCIS J. McELROY, A.B., J.C.L.
PRIEST OF THE ARCHDIOCESE OF PHILADELPHIA

THE CATHOLIC UNIVERSITY OF AMERICA PRESS
WASHINGTON, D. C.
1951

NIHIL OBSTAT:

JEROME D. HANNAN, A.M., LL.B., S.T.D., J.C.D.

Censor Deputatus

Washingtonii, die 12 aprilis, 1949

IMPRIMATUR:

✠ D. CARD. DOUGHERTY

Archiepiscopus Philadelphiensis

Philadelphiae, die 16 aprilis, 1949

MURRAY & HEISTER
WASHINGTON, D. C.

PRINTED BY
TIMES AND NEWS PUBLISHING CO.
GETTYSBURG, PA., U.S.A.

TO
MY MOTHER AND SISTER
and to
the memory of
MY FATHER

TABLE OF CONTENTS

TABLE OF CONTENTS (Continued)

PART TWO

FOREWORD

Divine Institution determines the position of Bishops in the Catholic Church, establishing them as successors of the Apostles and, in virtue of ordinary power, rulers of their diocese under the authority of the Roman Pontiff.[1]

As members of a divinely established hierarchy, Bishops enjoy personal privileges fittingly bestowed in recognition of their high position. They further enjoy the exercise of certain real privileges attached to the office of diocesan ordinary of which they may be incumbents.

The purpose of this work is to present a treatment of these privileges with emphasis upon their use. In the work the writer has restricted himself, in the main, to a consideration of the privileges granted to residential and titular Bishops by the Code of Canon Law. Consequently, no consideration has been given to private or particular privileges which Bishops may enjoy through indult or other grant. Likewise the extent of these privileges as affecting Archbishops has received no direct treatment in this work. Liturgical privileges as such have been handled when specifically mentioned in the Code, for example, the privilege of enjoying the assistance of a priest while offering the Holy Sacrifice of the Mass.[2] Otherwise liturgical problems such as the use of the *Pontificalia* or episcopal vestments do not come within the scope of this work.

The writer wishes on this occasion to express his gratitude to His Eminence, Dennis Cardinal Dougherty, Archbishop of Philadelphia, for the opportunity of advanced study; to the Faculty of the School of Canon Law for assistance in the preparation of this dissertation, and to all others who have in any way made this work possible.

---

[1] *Codex Iuris Canonici Pii X Pontificis Maximi iussu digestus Benedicti XV auctoritate promulgatus* (Romae: Typis Polyglottis Vaticanis, 1917), canon 329, § 1 (hereafter cited with the word canon).

[2] Canon 812.

CHAPTER I

Preliminary Remarks on Privileges and Bishops

ARTICLE I. THE NOTION OF PRIVILEGE

The term privilege as used in Canon Law has a twofold meaning, namely, a concession made in favor of an individual person, or even of a particular class or group of persons; and a particular or individual rule or benefit of law, granted to all those persons who are found in special conditions of life.[1] The law does not define a privilege. The commentators on canon law have not been in agreement on a definition. Vermeersch (1858-1936) Creusen[2] define privilege as a particular law which does not determine what is required, but grants a favor to persons either individually or as members of a group. Cappello[3] speaks of a privilege as particular law contained in the common law, by which special prerogatives are granted to persons, places, things, etc. Coronata[4] describes a privilege as a particular and favorable law legitimately constituted and promulgated in favor of a determined order or assembly of persons, or even in favor of places and things.

From a study of these definitions it appears that a privilege implies a divergence from the law, which may be either against or beyond the law. To allow for such a divergence the grantor

---

[1] Cicognani, *Canon Law* (2. revised ed., authorized English version by Rev. Joseph M. O'Hara and Rt. Rev. Msgr. Francis J. Brennan, Westminster: Newman Bookshop, 1946), p. 779.

[2] *Epitome Iuris Canonici* (3 vols., Mechliniae-Romae: H. Dessain, 1937-1946. Vol. I, 6. ed., 1937; Vol. II, 6. ed., 1940; Vol. III, 6. ed., 1946), I, n. 178 (hereafter cited *Epitome*).

[3] *Summa Iuris Canonici* (3 vols., Romae: Apud Aedes Universitatis Gregorianae, 1940-1945; Vols. I et II, 4. ed., 1945; Vol. III, 2. ed., 1940), I, n. 162 (hereafter cited *Summa*).

[4] *Institutiones Iuris Canonici ad Usum Utriusque Cleri et Scholarum* (5 vols., Romae: Marietti, 1936-1945; Vols. I et II, 2. ed., 1939; Vol. III, 2. ed., 1941; Vol. IV, 2. ed., 1945; Vol. V, 1936), I, n. 84 (hereafter cited *Institutiones*).

must enjoy competence.[5] The divergent disposition confers upon the grantee the right to actions which are either beyond or against the law. Thus the grantor must have competence to grant such rights through exemptions and special provisions. In view of these facts one may imply the definition of Roelker[6] and define a privilege as a concession of some special right as made by a competent superior.

Privileges may be granted through law itself or by way of particular indult.[7] The privileges of Bishops are examples of privileges granted through the law. The priest who celebrates Mass upon a portable altar, in virtue of his membership in the Catholic Near East Welfare Association, is making use of a privilege granted by way of particular indult.

As Bishops enjoy both personal and real privileges, it is necessary to consider this division of privileges. Real privileges are attached to some object, place or office. The right to use real privileges is conferred upon the person to whom the office, place or object belongs.[8] Bishops may hold the office of diocesan ordinary[9] to which are attached certain privileges, such as the granting of the Papal Benediction with a plenary indulgence.[10] Thus if a Bishop possesses this Office he enjoys the real privilege of granting the Papal Benediction in accordance with the terms of the Canon.

Personal privileges are granted to physical and moral persons. If privileges are granted directly in favor of a person because of his own merit they are *individually* personal. But if they are granted to some class of persons, the members of which enjoy the privileges

---

[5] Van Hove, *De Privilegiis, De Dispensationibus, Commentarium Lovaniense in Codicem Iuris Canonici* (Vol. I, tom. V, Mechliniae-Romae: Dessain, 1939), nn. 40, 41, 42 (hereafter cited *De Privilegiis*).

[6] *Principles of Privileges according to the Code of Canon Law,* The Catholic University of America Canon Law Studies, n. 35 (Washington, D. C.: The Catholic University of America, 1926), p. 16 (hereafter cited *Principles of Privilege*).

[7] Vermeersch-Creusen, *Epitome,* I, n. 179.

[8] Coronata, *Institutiones,* I, n. 87.

[9] Canon 334, § 1.

[10] Canon 914.

only because they belong to the class, they are *commonly* personal.[11] The greater number of Episcopal privileges are of this latter type.

The use of the Episcopal privileges, whether personal or real, depends upon the will of the individual Bishops, for they are not obligated to make use of them.[12] But they cannot renounce them as individuals[13] or as a body, since these privileges have the nature of law.[14] In fact, it would require a new general law to revoke them.[15]

The commonly personal privileges of the Episcopate may be used by a Bishop wherever he may happen to be.[16] The real Episcopal privileges may be used for the residential Bishop's subjects and for all others within the limits of his diocese.[17]

As clerics[18] Bishops also enjoy the general clerical privileges, inclusive of the exemption from military service and from civil service alien to the clerical state.[19]

However, the faithful are bound more strictly to observe the personal inviolability of a Bishop, than that of clerics of a lower rank.[20] In some judicial procedures a more extensive privileged forum has been extended to the Episcopate, than that reserved for clerics of a lower rank.[21]

ARTICLE II. THE NATURE AND THE DIVISIONS OF THE EPISCOPATE

The Episcopate is an office established by Divine Institution in so far as the power of the office is concerned. In this regard it can not be suppressed or supplanted, substantially changed or limited by the Roman Pontiff. However, the extent of this power was not

---

[11] Coronata, *Institutiones,* I, n. 87; Cicognani, *Canon Law,* pp. 781-782.
[12] Canon 69.
[13] Canon 72, § 3.
[14] Canon 72, § 4.
[15] Canon 71.
[16] Canon 74.
[17] Cf. canons 349, § 2, 2°; 914; 916.
[18] Canon 108.
[19] Canon 121.
[20] Canons 119; 2343: Teodori, "Privilegium Canonis-Consultationes"—*Apollinaris* (Romae, 1928-), V (1932), 115.
[21] Canon 1557, § 1, 3°; § 2, 1°.

determined in the Divine Institution. It is left, therefore, to the Holy See to define its limits with regard to subjects and territory.[22] This power which the Bishops enjoy as successors of the Apostles[23] is the ordinary apostolic power consisting of the fullness of the Sacrament of Orders and of Jurisdiction in a particular Diocese.[24] A Bishop, then, is a prelate who possesses the fullness of the priesthood together with jurisdiction in both forums by which he rules a particular diocese.[25] Titular Bishops are not comprehended under this definition. They do not possess jurisdiction, but in their consecration they do receive Episcopal powers. The use of these powers may become restricted through the fact that they have not taken canonical possession of their titular sees.[26]

As this work will consider the real and personal privileges of Bishops, it will be helpful to divide the various types of Bishops according to the classes which enjoy both the real and personal privileges, and the classes which enjoy the personal privileges alone.

Bishops are primarily classified as residential or titular. Residential Bishops or Bishops Ordinaries have both Episcopal Orders and actual jurisdiction over the clergy and laity of the diocese entrusted to them. Titular Bishops possess Episcopal Orders, but have no jurisdiction in virtue of their consecration even in their titular sees.[27] Titular Bishops are further classified. Coadjutors or

---

[22] Canon 215, § 1; Cappello, *Summa,* I, n. 360; Chelodi, *Ius de Personis* (2. ed., a Sac. Ernesto Bertagnolli, Tridenti Libr. edit. Tridentum, 1927), n. 186.

[23] Canon 329, § 1.

[24] The Apostles also enjoyed extraordinary powers of preaching everywhere, and of establishing churches, and of consecrating Bishops, etc.; Cappello, *Summa,* I, n. 361.

[25] Chelodi, *Ius De Personis,* n. 187.

[26] De Meester, *Juris Canonici et Juris Canonico-Civilis Compendium* (nova ed., 3 Vols. in 4, Brugis; Desclée, 1921-1928; Vol. I, 2. ed., 1921; Vol. II, 2. ed., 1923; Vol. III, pars I, 2. ed., 1926; Vol. III, pars II, 2. ed., 1928), II, n. 663 (hereafter cited *Compendium*).

[27] Wernz-Vidal, *Ius Canonicum* (7 Vols. in 9, Romae: Universitas Gregoriana, 1927-1946, Vol. I, 1938; Vol. II, 3. ed., a P. Philippo Aguirre recognita, 1943; Vol. III, 1933; Vol. IV, pars I, 1934; Vol. IV, pars II, 1935; Vol. V, 3. ed., a Philippo Aguirre recognita, 1946; Vol. VI, pars I, 1927; Vol. VI, pars II, 1928; Vol. VII, 1937), II, n. 572; Coronata, *Institutiones,* I, n. 402.

assistant Bishops are titular Bishops assigned by the Holy See to certain residential Bishops for the purpose of supplying the insufficiency or inability of these Bishops in the rule of their dioceses and in the exercise of Episcopal Orders.[28] These Coadjutors are rarely assigned to the see itself. It is customary that they be assigned to the person of the Bishop with the right of succession. If their assignment is to the person of the Bishop without the right of succession, they are known as auxiliary Bishops.[29] Further, titular Bishops may fill the office of Apostolic Administrator.[30] On the other hand, they may be purely titular Bishops, that is, Bishops not canonically assigned to an established see. In this latter group may be numbered retired residential Bishops, Apostolic Delegates, Papal Nuncios and others whose office of assisting the Pontiff in the apostolic ministry can be served more fittingly by one endowed with the Episcopal dignity.[31]

All Bishops without exception, residential and titular, enjoy the personal Episcopal privileges.[32] But only residential Bishops and titular Bishops with a status equal to that of residential Bishops have the use of real privileges attached to the office of Bishop

---

[28] Canons 350, §§ 1 and 2; 351, § 4; De Meester, *Compendium,* II, n. 704; Blat, *Commentarium Textus Codicis Iuris Canonici* (5 Vols. in 7, Romae: Apud Angelicum, 1921-1927, Lib. I, 1921; Lib. II, 2. ed., 1921; Lib. III, pars I, 2. ed., 1924; Lib. III, partes II-VI, 1923; Lib. IV, 1927; Lib. V, 1924), II, n. 378 (hereafter cited *Commentarium*); Cappello, *Summa,* I, n. 363; Vermeersch-Creusen, *Epitome,* I, n. 464; Lynch, *Coadjutors and Auxiliaries of Bishops,* The Catholic University of America Canon Law Studies, n. 238 (Washington, D. C.: The Catholic University of America Press, 1947), p. 36 (hereafter cited *Coadjutors*).

[29] Canon 350, §§ 2 and 3. In the United States, the majority of coadjutors are auxiliary Bishops. Cf. Lynch, *Coadjutors,* p. 35.

[30] The Code defines an Apostolic Administrator as a cleric to whom the Holy See, induced by special serious reasons, entrusts the government of a canonically erected diocese, *sede plena* or *sede vacante*—Canon 312.

[31] Smith, *Elements of Ecclesiastical Law Adapted especially to the Discipline of the Church in the United States* (3 Vol., New York: Benziger Brothers, 1887-1888; Vol. I, *Ecclesiastical Persons,* 9. ed., 1887), I, 394 (hereafter cited as *Elements of Law*).

[32] Canons 349, § 1, 1°; 812; etc.

Ordinary. Coadjutors granted to a totally incapacitated Bishop[33] have all Episcopal rights and duties.[34] Titular Bishops who are permanent Apostolic Administrators are bound by the same obligations and enjoy the same rights and honors as the Bishop Ordinary.[35] Both the Coadjutor of a totally incapacitated Bishop and the permanent Apostolic Administrator in assuming all power ordinarily held by a residential Bishop have a status equal to his, and hence are entitled to make use of the real privileges of a Bishop Ordinary.[36]

In accordance with the division of personal and real Episcopal privileges, this work will be divided into two parts. The first part will contain a discussion of the personal privileges which all Bishops enjoy in virtue of their Episcopal dignity. The second part will consider the real privileges which Bishops as Ordinaries are entitled to use.

---

[33] The words "totally incapacited" are a translation of the Latin words, "*Prorsus inhabilis*" of canon 351, § 2, which at least refer to a Bishop disabled for the performance of human acts. Lynch gives a full treatment of this phrase. Cf. Lynch, *Coadjutors*, p. 73.

[34] Canon 351, § 2.

[35] Canon 315, § 1.

[36] Lynch, *Coadjutors*, p. 76; McDonough, *Apostolic Administrators*, The Catholic University of America Canon Law Studies, n. 139 (Washington, D. C.: The Catholic University of America Press, 1941), pp. 162 ff.; Vermeersch-Creusen, *Epitome*, I, n. 381; Coronata, *Institutiones*, I, n. 346.

PART I

Personal Privileges Common to All Bishops

CHAPTER II

Privileges Centering About the Holy Sacrifice of the Mass

ARTICLE I. GENERAL INTRODUCTION TO PART ONE

The personal privileges common to all Bishops are referred to in canon 349, § 1, 1°. This canon refers to the privileges of Cardinals mentioned in canon 239, § 1, 2° to 12°, which Bishops enjoy with some limitation, as well as the privileges contained under different titles in the Code and found in the following canons: 811, § 2; 812; 1166, § 3; 1189; 1401; 1557, § 1, 2°; 1770, § 2, 1°; 2227, §2.

All Bishops, both residential and titular, are granted the use of these privileges from the time they receive authentic notification of their promotion to the Episcopate.[1] This notification is usually made in the form of an apostolic bull or brief,[2] upon the reception of which a priest, though he lack Episcopal consecration, may, for example, celebrate anywhere upon a portable altar, bless rosaries, medals, etc. The requisite for the immediate use of these privileges is not Episcopal consecration but the reception of the bull of appointment.[3]

Since these privileges are bestowed in view of the Episcopal character actually possessed or about to be received[4] they are purely personal. The fact of their exclusive personal nature is supported by two replies of the Sacred Penitentiary—the first forbidding

---

[1] Canon 349, § 1.

[2] Wernz-Vidal, *Ius Canonicum*, II, n. 597.

[3] S.C. Consist., 2 maii 1920—*Acta Apostolicae Sedis, Commentarium Officiale* (Romae, 1909-1929); Civitate Vaticana, 1929-), XII (1920), 371 (hereafter cited as *AAS*).

[4] Vermeersch, "Consultationes"—*Periodica de Religiosis et Missionariis* (Brugis, 1905-1919); *Periodica de Re Canonica et Morali utili praesertim Religiosis et Missionariis*, 1920-1927; *Periodica de Re Canonica, Morali, Liturgica*, 1927-), X (1922), 95 (hereafter cited *Periodica*); S.R.C., 26 nov. 1919, V, ad 2—*AAS*, XII (1920), 180-182.

habitual delegation of the faculties of canon 349, § 1,[5] the second forbidding the delegation of the same faculties in individual cases (*per modum actus*) being specific in mentioning that the Vicar General, as such, did not enjoy them.[6]

ARTICLE II. THE PRIVILEGE OF OFFERING A PRIVATE MASS ON HOLY THURSDAY AND OF CELEBRATING SUCCESSIVELY FROM MIDNIGHT THREE MASSES ON CHRISTMAS

The Church has carefully determined the time for offering the Holy Sacrifice of the Mass. It allows the celebration of Mass on all days of the year except those that are excluded by the proper rite of the celebrant.[7] In general, all private Masses[8] are forbidden in the Latin rite on Holy Thursday.[9] This prohibition was established before the Code by the Sacred Congregation of Rites.[10] However, by way of exception, Bishops enjoy the privilege of celebrating or having celebrated in their presence a private Mass on this day.[11] The general law further allows the celebration of one Mass at midnight, Christmas, in all parochial and conventual churches. An apostolic indult is required in order to continue with the immediate celebration of one or both of the other Masses of the Christmas Liturgy.[12] Again, Bishops enjoy a privilege of exemp-

---

[5] 18 iul. 1919—*AAS,* XI (1919), 332.

[6] 10 nov. 1926—*AAS,* XVIII (1926), 500. A Vicar General who is a Bishop would of course enjoy these faculties.

[7] Canon 823, § 1: Mass may not be offered on Good Friday in the Latin rite.

[8] A private Mass differs from a public Mass in this that it is not celebrated because of a public need or a juridical obligation, but rather for the private devotion of those present, or of the celebrant, or for some other private reasons—O'Connell, *The Celebration of Mass* (3 vols., Milwaukee: Bruce Publishing Co., 1940-1941), I, 274.

[9] "Triduo sequenti prohibentur omnes Missae privatae," Rubric at end of Mass for Wednesday of Holy Week—*Missale Romanum.*

[10] S.R.C., *Urbis,* 28 mart. 1775, ad V—*Decreta Authentica Congregationis Sacrorum Rituum* (5 vols., Romae: ex Typographia Polyglotta, 1898-1901; Appendix I, 1912; Appendix II, 1927), n. 2503 (hereafter cited *Decr. Auth.*); S.R.C., Resolutionis Dubiorum, 28 iul. 1821—*Decr. Auth.,* n. 2616.

[11] Canons 349, § 1, 1°, and 239, § 1, 4°.

[12] Canon 821, § 2.

tion from this law. They may celebrate or have another celebrate in their presence three Masses successively at midnight on Christmas Day.

In the use of this privilege of celebrating a private Mass on Holy Thursday, titular Bishops, as such, are themselves permitted to celebrate or have another priest celebrate for them. But residential Bishops and titular Bishops with a status equal to that of residential Bishops, namely the Coadjutor of a totally incapacitated Bishop and the permanent Apostolic Administrator[13] are limited in the use of this privilege by the clause, *"Dummodo non teneantur celebrare in cathedrali,"* of canon 349, § 1, 1°. It is difficult to determine the exact import of this clause. There are two possible interpretations. One interpretation teaches that, when the bishop is bound to celebrate in his cathedral, he does not enjoy this privilege, and may not then have another priest celebrate for him. Vermeersch-Creusen[14] and Toso[15] support this interpretation. The other interpretation teaches that, when the Bishop is bound to offer the Holy Sacrifice in his cathedral, he may still make use of the privilege of having another priest offer the Masses allowed by the privilege. Coronata,[16] whom Hynes[17] follows, supports this latter interpretation. Cappello[18] does not consider the problem whether or not the Bishop who is bound to celebrate in his cathedral

---

[13] The permanent Apostolic Administrator is always a Bishop, whether titular or a neighboring residential Bishop. Cf. Toso, *Ad Codicem Iuris Canonici Commentaria Minora* (5 vols., Romae: Marietti, 1920-1934; Vol. II, tom. I, 1922; Vol. II, tom. II, 1923), Lib. II, tom. II, p. 137 (hereafter cited *Commentaria*); Wernz-Vidal, *Ius Canonicum,* II, n. 599; McDonough, *Apostolic Administrators,* pp. 114, 121, 161.

[14] *Epitome,* II, n. 97.

[15] *Commentaria,* Lib. II, tom. II, p. 180.

[16] *Institutiones,* I, n. 401.

[17] *The Privileges of Cardinals,* The Catholic University of America Canon Law Studies, n. 217 (Washington, D. C.: The Catholic University of America Press, 1945), p. 79.

[18] *Summa,* I, n. 388; *Tractatus Canonico-Moralis de Sacramentis iuxta Codicem Iuris Canonici* (5 vols., Romae: Marietti, 1942-1947; Vol. I, 4. ed., 1945; Vol. II, 4. ed., 1944; Vol. III, 2. ed., 1942; Vol. IV, editio altera accurate recognita et aucta, 1947; Vol. V, 5. ed., 1947), I, n. 737 (hereafter cited *De Sacramentis*).

can permit another priest to celebrate the Masses allowed by this privilege.

The better interpretation depends in part on whether or not the clause, *"dummodo non teneantur celebrare in cathedrali,"* sets an essential condition for the use of the privilege. Canon 39, on rescripts, indicates that clauses introduced by *"dummodo"* imply essential conditions in a rescript. It makes clauses, thus introduced, essential conditions that need be fulfilled before the rescript may be used.[19] Using this as a norm in the present case, a Bishop would not enjoy this privilege whenever he is bound to celebrate in his cathedral on the days mentioned in the privilege. From this it follows that he, likewise, would not be permitted to allow another priest to celebrate for him on such days. This seems to be the better interpretation. For it is difficult to see how this privilege, apparently granted to Bishops for their personal convenience on Holy Thursday and Christmas Day, would serve their convenience by permitting them to have another celebrate for them on these days, when they themselves are bound to offer Mass in their cathedrals. Further, this interpretation is more in accord with the very nature of a privilege, which is that of granting a favor.[20]

When the Bishop is bound to offer Mass in the cathedral, the privilege is rendered nugatory in his regard, since the very favor which it grants is impossible of realization because of the Bishop's obligation. It likewise does not seem to grant him the favor which would allow him to delegate another priest for the celebration of the Masses regarding which provision is made in the privilege. In view of this the clause, *"dummodo non teneantur celebrare in cathedrali,"* seems to point to an essential condition for the use of the privilege itself, and to indicate that the Bishop does not enjoy the use of this privilege whenever he is bound to celebrate in his cathedral on the days covered by the privilege.

The next problem is to determine whether or not Bishops Ordinary are bound to celebrate Mass in their cathedrals on Holy Thursday and on Christmas Day. On Holy Thursday, since the Holy Oils must be blessed at Mass, there can be no doubt about

---

[19] Vermeersch-Creusen, *Epitome,* I, n. 159; Cappello, *Summa,* I, n. 149.

[20] Van Hove, *De Privilegiis,* n. 176.

the obligation of Bishops Ordinary to offer the Holy Sacrifice in the cathedral.[21] Hence on Holy Thursday, residential Bishops do not enjoy the use of the privilege herein considered, not even with regard to giving another priest permission to celebrate for them.

In considering the use of this privilege on Christmas Day it must be noted that residential Bishops are required to be at their cathedrals on that day.[22] It must be noted further that the *Bishops' Ceremonial*[23] list the Feast of the Nativity among the days for the celebration of Pontifical Mass. These facts would lead one to think that residential Bishops are bound to celebrate a Pontifical Mass in their cathedrals on Christmas Day. However, Catalanus (+ after 1759)[24] and Moretti,[25] in speaking of this section of the *Bishops' Ceremonial,* point out that the listing in the *Ceremonial* serves to indicate the days on which it is fitting to hold pontifical functions, and not the days on which pontifical functions are necessarily of obligation. Hence, since the Code of Canon Law requires nothing other than presence of the residential Bishops in their cathedrals on Christmas Day, it would be safe to follow the opinion of the authors mentioned in interpreting the law of the *Ceremonial* and conclude that residential Bishops are not bound to the celebration of the Nativity Masses in their cathedrals. Thus they may use this privilege by celebrating themselves or by having

---

[21] Canon 734, § 1; Nabuco, *Pontificalis Romani Expositio Juridico-Practica* (3 vols., Petropoli-Brasilia: Sumptibus Editōria Vozes, LTDA, 1945), III, nn. 5 and 6 (hereafter cited *Pontificalis Expositio*); Catalanus, *Caeremoniale Episcoporum in Duos Libros Distributum, Clementis VIII et Innocentii X nunc primum Commentariis Illustratum* (Paris: Sumptibus A. Jouby, 1860), II, 518 (hereafter cited *Caeremoniale Episcoporum*); Coronata, *Institutiones,* I, n. 401; Toso, *Commentaria,* Lib. II, tom. II, p. 180.

[22] Canon 338, § 3.

[23] *Caeremoniale Episcoporum Clementis VIII, Innocentii X, et Benedicti XIII iussu editum, Benedicti XIV et Leonis XIII auctoritate recognitum, ed. Typica* (New York: Fr. Pustet & Co., 1886), Lib. II, cap. XXXIV, nn. 1-3.

[24] *Caeremoniale Episcoporum,* II, 518, 519.

[25] *Caeremoniale iuxta Ritum Romanum seu de Sacris Functionibus, Episcopo Celebrante-Assistente-Absente* (4 vols., Taurini: Marietti, 1936-1939; Vol. I, 1936; Vol. II, 1937; Vol. III, 1938; Vol. IV, 1939), I, n. 118 (hereafter cited *De Sacris Functionibus*).

another celebrate in their presence, at midnight, the three Masses allowed by the Christmas liturgy.

Now, all Bishops in celebrating the Christmas Masses according to this privilege are free to celebrate either one or two of the Christmas Masses at midnight. For a privilege which concedes the more extensive favor of celebrating three Masses at midnight certainly concedes also the less extensive favor of celebrating one or two Masses under the same circumstances.[26] For the same reason the priest who celebrates at midnight, Christmas, at the Bishop's request, may offer one or two Masses according as he is requested by the Bishop.

At this point the question may be asked, "May a Bishop residential or titular who celebrates Mass at midnight, Christmas, in a cathedral or parish church continue immediately with the celebration of the remaining Masses of Christmas?" The authors consulted do not deal directly with this problem.[26a] Canon 821, § 2 seems to indicate that the answer should be in the negative. However, the writer ventures an affirmative answer for the following reasons. Some authors[26b] and the Sacred Congregation of Rites[26c] claim that for a just reason any celebrant of the Christmas Midnight Mass may continue with the immediate celebration of the other Masses of the Feast. The existence of the Episcopal privilege in this matter appears to be reason enough for any Bishop to continue with the celebration of the other Christmas Masses once he has celebrated, at midnight, in a cathedral or parish church.

---

[26] "Cui licet quod est plus, licet utique quod est minus."—Reg. 53, R.J., in VI°; Coronata, *Institutiones Iuris Canonici ad Usum Utriusque Cleri et Scholarum, de Sacramentis, Tractatus Canonicus* (3 vols., Romae: Marietti, 1943-1946; Vol. I, 1943; Vol. II, 1945; Vol. III, 1946), I, n. 235, p. 202 (hereafter cited *De Sacramentis*).

[26a] E.g., Blat, *Commentarium,* II, n. 205; Chelodi, *Ius de Personis,* n. 195 (c); Regatillo, *Ius Sacramentarium* (2 vols., Santander: Sal Terrae, 1945-1946; Vol. I, 1945; Vol. II, 1946), I, n. 189; Claeys Bouuaert, F.—Simenon, *Manuale Juris Canonici* (3 vols., Vols. I and III, 3 ed., Vol. II, 1. ed., Gandae et Leodii: Dessain, 1930-1931), I, n. 490; Vermeersch-Creusen, *Epitome,* II, n. 97.

[26b] Cappello, *De Sacramentis,* I, n. 742; Coronata, *De Sacramentis,* I, n. 235.

[26c] *Decr.* 18 sept. 1781—*Decr. Auth.,* n. 1520.

Moreover, the privilege itself does not limit its use as to place. Accordingly, to deny a Bishop residential or titular the right to celebrate the Three Masses in a cathedral or parish church at midnight, Christmas, appears as a restriction of the privilege, which restriction seems ruled out by the general law regarding the interpretation of privileges.[26d]

Another question arises as to whether or not a Bishop who has celebrated at midnight, Christmas, in a cathedral or parish church may return to his oratory and there celebrate immediately the remaining Masses of the Feast. There seems to be no reason for forbidding this practice as the privilege is not limited in its use to a certain place.

This privilege is not primarily concerned with the faculty of celebrating the three Masses of Christmas at midnight, but rather with the right of granting this faculty to certain individuals, namely to the Bishop or the priest chosen by the Bishop. Hence it may not be used in such fashion that the Bishop himself would celebrate one or two of the Masses and then have another celebrate the remaining Mass or Masses which the privilege contemplates.[27] Further, the faculty of this privilege entitles *either* the Bishop *or* the priest chosen by the Bishop to celebrate the three Masses. It does not provide that both may celebrate.[28] For as Hynes[29] points out, an argument in favor of the allowable act of celebration on the part of both can not be deduced from the use of the disjunctive particle "*vel*" in the canon which accords the privilege.[30]

In classical Latinity, the particle "*vel*" does indeed signify the one or the other, or both; "*aut,*" the one or the other, not both. However, the Code uses these interchangeably, and thus it seems warranted to hold that *vel* was used with the meaning of *aut,* especially in view of the fact that this privilege is given in recognition of the Episcopal dignity. Further, the grant of the portable altar, in

[26d] Canon 67—Privilegium ex ipsius tenore aestimandum est, *nec licet illud extendere aut restringere.* (Italics are the author's.)

[27] Blat, *Commentarium,* II, n. 205.

[28] Blat, *loc. cit.;* Toso, *Commentaria,* Lib. II, tom. II, p. 38; O'Connell, *The Celebration of Mass,* I, 39.

[29] *The Privileges of Cardinals,* pp. 79, 80.

[30] Cf. canon 239, § 1, 4°.

indicating that two Masses may be said, makes its statement in clear and unequivocal language.[31] In view of these points the privilege is best interpreted as allowing *either* the Bishop *or* another priest to celebrate. It does not allow both to celebrate.

By force of this privilege all Bishops may celebrate three Masses successively at midnight, Christmas, or select another priest to celebrate these Masses in their presence. On Holy Thursday, however, only those Bishops who are not consecrating the Holy Oils may celebrate privately or select another to offer in their presence the private Mass which this privilege allows to be celebrated.

ARTICLE III. THE PRIVILEGE OF USING A PORTABLE ALTAR

The privilege of a portable altar entitles the grantee to celebrate Mass outside of a church or oratory on a consecrated altar stone.[32] This privilege is obtained either by way of indult or through the general law. The granting of it is reserved to the Apostolic See.[33] The Code itself entitles Bishops to use the portable altar.[34]

Pope Boniface VIII (1294-1303) first established in the general law the Bishop's privilege of a portable altar.[35] However, early in the history of the Church Bishops alowed others to use the portable altar.[36] They also used it for their own convenience. Gattico (1704-

---

[31] Canon 239, § 1, 7°: ". . . et permittendi ut alia Missa, ipsis adstantibus, celebretur."

[32] Gasparri, *Tractatus Canonicus de Sanctissima Eucharistia* (2 vols., Parisiis et Lugduni, 1897), I, n. 261 (hereafter cited *De Eucharistia*); Coronata, *De Sacramentis,* I, n. 257, p. 227.

[33] Canon 822, § 2.

[34] Canons 349, § 1, 1° and 239, § 1, 7°.

[35] "Quoniam episcopi eorumque superiores se habent diversis ex causis a suis ecclesiis et dioecesibus absentare frequenter, nec semper possunt commode ad ecclesias accedere pro missa celebranda vel audienda in ipsis, sine qua eos transire non decet absque causa rationabili ullam diem: praesenti constitutione indulgemus eisdem, ut altare possint habere viaticum, et in eo celebrare ac facere celebrari, ubicumque absque interdicti transgressione illis permittitur celebrare vel audire divina."—c. 12, *de privilegiis,* V, 7, in VI°.

[36] Dionysius of Alexandria granted such a permission around the year 255—Eusebius, *Ecclesiastical History,* Lib. VII, cap. 22—Migne, *Patrologiae Cursus Completus, Series Graeca* (161 vols., Parisiis, 1856-1866), XX, 688

1754) listed reports, as early as of the third century, of Bishops who used portable altars for Mass when they were sick or traveling.[37]

The reason for Pope Boniface's action may have been his desire to give to the Bishops the same privilege of a portable altar which the Friars Minor and members of the Order of Preachers already enjoyed in virtue of a grant by Pope Honorius III (1216-1227).[38] But the more cogent reason seems to have been that the Pontiff thought it necessary to guarantee to the Bishops their right to the unrestricted use of the portable altar by means of a papal law. For in his time some of the Bishops of Europe and England, in their zeal for restricting the celebration of Mass to churches and oratories, were preventing Bishops from using a portable altar while traveling.[39]

The Council of Trent (1545-1563) indirectly withdrew the portable altar privileges by legislating that Mass could be offered only in a church or an oratory.[40] However, this legislation did not affect the Episcopal right to the use of the portable altar, as is borne out by subsequent decisions of the Sacred Congregation of

---

(hereafter cited *MPG*); St. Augustine tells of Mass being celebrated in the home of a sick family with the permission of the Bishop—St. Augustinus, *De Civitate Dei,* Lib. XXII, cap. 8—*Corpus Scriptorum Ecclesiasticorum Latinorum* (Vindobonae, 1866—), XXXX, pars. II, p. 602 (hereafter cited as *CSEL*).

[37] *De Oratoriis Domesticis et de Usu Altaris Portatilis* (Romae, 1747), pp. 388, 389, nn. II, III (hereafter cited *De Oratoriis*).

[38] *Bullarium Ordinis Praedicatorum,* I (Romae, 1729), p. 14, n. 24; Potthast, *Regesta Pontificum Romanorum inde ab A. post Christum natum 1198 ad A. 1304* (2 vols., Berolini, 1874-1875), n. 6654 (hereafter cited Potthast); *Bullarium Franciscanorum,* I (Romae, 1759), p. 20, n. 17; Potthast, n. 7325.

[39] Gattico, *De Oratoriis,* p. 389, n. IV.

[40] Sess. XXII, *de Sacrificio Missae,* c. 9, *de abservandis et evitandis in celebratione missae*—Schroeder, *Canons and Decrees of the Council of Trent* (St. Louis: B. Herder Book Co., 1941), p. 423 (hereafter cited *Council of Trent*); Bliley, *Altars according to the Code of Canon Law,* The Catholic University of America Canon Law Studies, n. 38 (Washington, D. C.: The Catholic University of America, 1922), p. 48 (hereafter cited *Altars*).

Cardinals for the Interpretation of Council of Trent.[41] The decision of February 18, 1623, clearly stated that Bishops had the right to use the portable altar, as granted by Boniface VIII, without obtaining the permission of any diocesan Ordinary.[42]

Though the privilege remained in force after the Council of Trent, Pope Clement XI (1700-1721) in 1703 restricted the use of the portable altar to the Bishop's own residence, and forbade its use in the homes of the laity either in or outside of the Bishop's diocese.[43] In this way he hoped to overcome the abuse that had developed in the use of this privilege. In 1723 Pope Innocent XIII (1721-1724) approved the action of Clement XI. But he applied to it an interpretation more in accord with the original grant of Boniface, by allowing Bishops the use of the portable altar when making the diocesan visitation, when living outside their diocese with the permission of the Holy See, and while staying as a guest in the home of a layman.[44]

The use of the privilege was conditioned on nothing else than that the Bishop have a reason for using the portable altar. Thus, even a visit to the home of a friend provided a sufficient reason.[45]

These regulations, however, are no longer in force,[46] as they are left unmentioned in the Code.[47] However, prudence seems to recommend their general observance to Bishops.[48]

Before the Code, the right of titular Bishops to enjoy the privilege of the portable altar was questioned. A reply of the Sacred Congregation of Rites vindicated this privilege for them.[49] Pope Leo

[41] E.g., S.C.C. *Florentina,* 23 maii 1615—*Codicis Iuris Canonici Fontes cura Eñi Petri Card. Gasparri editi* (9 vols., Romae, postea Civitate Vaticana: Typis Polyglottis Vaticanis, 1923-1939 [Vols. VII, VIII, IX ed. cura et studio Eñi Iustiniani Card. Seredi]), n. 2396 (hereafter cited *Fontes*).

[42] *Fontes,* n. 2436; Gattico, *De Oratoriis,* pp. 462 seq.

[43] Decr. Nonnulli, 15 dec. 1703—*Fontes,* n. 264.

[44] Innocentius XIII const. *Apostolici ministerii,* 23 maii 1723—*Fontes,* n. 280.

[45] De Angelis, *Praelectiones Iuris Canonici* (3 vols., Romae: Desclée, 1908), II, 299-301 (hereafter cited *Praelectiones*) ; Gasparri, *De Eucharistia,* I, n. 267.

[46] Cappello, *De Sacramentis,* I, n. 718.

[47] Canon 239, § 1, 7°.

[48] Bliley, *Altars,* p. 114.

[49] 22 aug. 1818—*Decr. Auth.,* n. 4547.

XIII (1878-1903) definitely stated that all Bishops, titular as well as residential had the right to use the portable altar.[50] Thus, even before the Code the privilege was interpreted in substantially the same fashion as it was when first granted by Pope Boniface VIII.

The privilege of the portable altar as conferred on all Bishops by the Code gives them the right of offering the Holy Sacrifice outside of churches and public or semi-public oratories that are consecrated or blessed for divine worship.[51] It is more extensive than the similar privilege of a domestic oratory in that it makes possible the celebration of Mass in all places, even those not specifically reserved for divine worship.[52] The clause, *"ubicumque degunt"* allows the use of the portable altar in any place, whether it be in a building, in the open air, or under the ground.[53] The general law forbids its use at sea,[54] but gives the Bishops another privilege whereby they may celebrate while traveling aboard ship.[55] This privilege will be considered in the next article.

Any place may be chosen for erecting the portable altar, provided that the place chosen be clean and becoming for the celebration of Mass.[56] This limitation naturally excludes any place in which there may be danger of profanation for the Holy Sacrifice.[57] Within these limits, however, Bishops may erect a portable altar and celebrate Mass thereon, in any diocese, even in the homes of the laity.[58]

It may be asked if a Bishop could celebrate Mass aboard a train while making a rail journey of several days' duration. Coronata[59] holds that the law of the portable altar does not prohibit its use

---

[50] S.R.C., *Urbis et Orbis,* 8 iun. 1896—*Fontes,* n. 6261.

[51] Coronata, *De Sacramentis,* I, n. 257.

[52] Coronata, *De Locis et Temporibus Sacris* (Augustae Taurinorum: Marietti, 1922), n. 123.

[53] Cappello, *De Sacramentis,* I, n. 718, 7; Coronata, *loc. cit.*

[54] Canon 822, § 3.

[55] Canons 349, § 1, 1° and 239, § 1, 8°.

[56] Cappello, *De Sacramentis,* I, n. 718.

[57] Coronata, *De Sacramentis,* I, n. 257.

[58] S.C.C. 18 febr. 1623—*Fontes,* n. 2436; Coronata, *De Locis et Temporibus Sacris,* n. 124, p. 126.

[59] *De Sacramentis,* I, n. 257, pp. 228, 229.

on trains. Cappello[60] holds the same opinion. Vermeersch-Creusen,[61] though they do not object to this opinion, think that an apostolic indult would be required for such celebration if the matter were brought to the attention of the Sacred Congregation of Rites. The writer follows the opinion of Coronata and Cappello, and maintains that a Bishop may celebrate and permit a priest to celebrate Mass in his presence while traveling on a train. For a railroad coach can certainly be a suitable place for offering the Holy Sacrifice, and this is all that the law requires for the use of a portable altar.[62]

In the matter of celebrating Mass while traveling by air, the writer is of the opinion that the general law would prohibit the Bishop from celebrating while making such a trip. For the unevenness of flight would certainly be a constant source of danger of profanation to the Sacred Species. The Code has not provided for the contingency of air travel and this omission on the part of the Code has not been supplied by any subsequent decree. Thus it would seem unwise for a Bishop to celebrate in an airplane without an indult from the Sacred Congregation of Rites.[63] In support of this view it may be noted that when Father Paul Schulte, O.M.I., celebrated Mass in the *Hindenburg,* he obtained permission from the Holy See through the Apostolic Nuncio at Berlin.[64]

Further, as regards the place in which this privilege may be used, Cappello[65] excludes the employment of a portable altar in a bedroom. Regatillo,[66] who in general holds the same opinion as Cappello, teaches that Bishops may use the portable altar in a bedroom, since the specific privilege of a portable altar as enjoyed by Bishops

---

[60] *De Sacramentis,* I, n. 712.

[61] *Epitome,* II, n. 101.

[62] Cf. "Cases and Studies"—*The Jurist* (Washington, D. C., 1941-), VIII (1948), 70.

[63] Vermeersch-Creusen, *Epitome,* I, n. 101; "Cases and Studies"—*The Jurist,* VIII (1948), 71.

[64] Cf. Bouscaren, *The Canon Law Digest* (2 vols., Milwaukee: Bruce Publishing Co., Vol. I, 1934; Vol. II, 1943), II, 203 (hereafter cited *Digest*).

[65] *De Sacramentis,* I, n. 718, 7.

[66] *Ius Sacramentarium,* I, n. 219. The writer refers the reader to this section of the work of Regatillo for a more thorough treatment of the reasons, both for and against the use of a portable altar in a bedroom.

is an exception to the law made in favor of Bishops in consideration of their dignity. This reason of Regatillo does not seem convincing for the Bishop's privilege in this matter seems certainly to be contemplated within the framework of the general law requirement that the place chosen for the celebration of Mass be suitable and decent.

Regatillo speaks as though the Bishop's privilege was an exception to this requirement. The writer maintains that the Bishop may indeed use the portable altar in a bedroom, but for the following reason. The disputed clause which forbids the celebration of Mass in a bedroom is directly attached to the statement which deals with the permission which can be granted *per modum actus* by the Ordinary.[67] This permission is primarily concerned with the authorization for the celebration of Mass outside of a church or oratory and only indirectly, if at all, does it relate to the use of the privilege of a portable altar. The only apparent connection is the necessity of using a portable altar in celebrating Mass outside of a church or oratory. This certainly is not the privilege of a portable altar as such. Hence, it is the Ordinaries granting of permission for the celebration of Mass in a bedroom that is forbidden. It is not the use of a portable altar in a bedroom that is specifically forbidden. Therefore, if the Holy See grants the privilege of a portable altar without limitation as it does in the case of Bishops,[68] the use of the portable altar in a bedroom does not seem precluded.[69] However, the general law would preclude the use of a bedroom if the room itself were unbecoming for the celebration of Mass.[70]

Bishops certainly may use this privilege in a domestic or private oratory. However, they do not enjoy the privilege conferred on Cardinals by force of which the indult of the oratory remains intact; and the usual daily Mass may be read on the same day and in

[67] Canon 822, § 4.

[68] Canons 349, § 1, 1° and 239, § 1, 7°—Celebrandi super aram portatilem non solum in domo propriae habitationis, *sed ubicumque degunt;* . . . Italics are the writer's.

[69] Bliley, *Altars,* p. 111; Coronata, *De Locis et Temporibus Sacris,* n. 124.

[70] Canon 822, § 3; Bevilacqua, *De Episcopi seu Ordinarii ex Novo Codice Canonico Iuribus ac Obligationibus* (New York: Fr. Pustet & Co., 1921), n. 623 (hereafter cited as *De Episcopi Iuribus*).

the same domestic or private oratory in which a Cardinal has already celebrated or will celebrate.[71] In using the portable altar privilege in a domestic or private oratory, the Bishops may even have another priest celebrate a second Mass in their presence in the oratory. If the oratory enjoys an Apostolic indult which provides for the celebration of one Mass daily,[72] no other priest may use the oratory for Mass on the same day on which a Bishop or the priest chosen by him celebrates therein. Coronata,[73] alone among the authors consulted, holds that Bishops implicitly enjoy the afore mentioned privilege of Cardinals, in as much as Bishops are permitted by privilege to use the portable altar everywhere. However, this opinion seems only conditionally tenable for the indults of domestic oratories usually allow the celebration of only one Mass.[74] This concession of the indult is verified in its use even when the Mass has been celebrated in a domestic oratory by some one who enjoyed the privilege of a portable altar. Hence when a Bishop has celebrated Mass in an oratory wherein the celebration of but one Mass is made allowable by the indult, then no other Mass may be read on the same day and in the same oratory in which the Bishop has already celebrated his Mass. The indult of the oratory would certainly not prevent the Bishop from having another Mass offered in his presence as he is allowed this by his privilege of a portable altar. But this would be the only case in which a second Mass could be offered in an oratory enjoying such an indult.

Should it happen that a Bishop wishes to celebrate in a domestic oratory after Mass had already been said therein by virtue of the indult which favors the oratory, he may do so. For authors are agreed that the privilege of a portable altar grants the faculty of offering the Holy Sacrifice anywhere outside of churches and public or semi-public oratories that are consecrated or blessed for divine worship.[75] Hence Bishops, in virtue of their portable altar

[71] Canon 239, § 1, 14°. Sacrum celebrandi in quolibet privato sacello sine praeiudicio illius qui indulto gaudet. Cf. Hynes, *The Privileges of Cardinals,* pp. 69, 70.

[72] Canon 1195, § 1.

[73] *De Locis et Temporibus Sacris,* n. 94.

[74] Vermeersch-Creusen, *Epitome,* II, n. 502.

[75] Coronata, *De Sacramentis,* I, n. 257; Cappello, *De Sacramentis,* I, n. 718; Gasparri, *De Eucharistia,* I, n. 257.

privilege may celebrate in domestic oratories after the Mass allowed by the indult has already been celebrated.

This doctrine seems further supported by the ruling of canon 67, which legislates that a privilege is to be neither extended nor restricted. To prohibit a Bishop from celebrating in a domestic oratory after the permissively authorized Mass has already been said would imply a restriction of the Bishop's portable altar privilege which allows him to celebrate Mass in any suitable and becoming place outside of a church, or a public or a semi-public oratory. A domestic oratory is certainly such a place. So it is in this latter sense that one can agree with Coronata in holding that Bishops implicitly enjoy the Cardinal's privilege of celebrating Mass in a domestic or private oratory without prejudice to the indult of the owner of the oratory.

The privilege of a portable altar allows for its use on all days of the year on which Mass may be celebrated. Bishops, then, may celebrate on a portable altar every day of the year except on Good Friday. They may celebrate Mass on a portable altar on Holy Thursday whenever by privilege they may celebrate Mass privately on that day. On Good Friday Mass may not be celebrated, and on Holy Saturday only one Mass is allowed in each parochial and conventual church.[76] Since it is most rare that the Sacred Congregation of Rites allows the celebration of a private Mass on Holy Saturday,[77] and since Bishops do not enjoy the privilege of celebrating privately on that day,[78] it follows conclusively that on Holy

---

[76] Rubric at the end of Mass for Wednesday of Holy Week—cf. *Missale Romanum;* Coronata, *De Sacramentis,* I, nn. 231, 232; Vermeersch-Creusen, *Epitome,* II, n. 95.

[77] Davis, *Moral and Pastoral Theology* (4. ed., 4 vol., New York: Sheed & Ward, 1943), III, 137, 138 (hereafter cited *Moral Theology*); Cappello, *De Sacramentis,* I, n. 738.

[78] Bishops may hold ordinations in their oratories on Holy Saturday.—S.R.C., resp. 21 mart. 1744, ad I—*Decr. Auth.,* n. 2375; Coronata, *De Sacramentis,* I, n. 232; Cappello, *De Sacramentis,* I, n. 738, p. 699. The Mass celebrated for these ordinations would not involve the privilege of the portable altar. For the Bishop's oratory has the rights and privileges of a semi-public oratory—canon 1189—and the privilege of a portable altar is concerned with celebration of Mass outside of such oratories.

Saturday as well as on Good Friday the use of the privilege of the portable altar may not be invoked by Bishops.

The privilege of the portable altar gives the Bishop the added right of having another priest celebrate for Him or after him in any of the circumstances described above.[79] This extension as contained in the original grant of Pope Boniface VIII[80] (1294-1303), is granted primarily to the person of the Bishop, since the priest in question must always celebrate in the presence of the Bishop, and may not celebrate in virtue of this extension if the Bishop be absent.[81] Moreover, this extension allows only one Mass in addition to the one celebrated by the Bishop. It does not allow several priests to celebrate, even though the Bishop be present.[82] To allow several priests to celebrate Mass on the portable altar would be an illegal extension which is forbidden by the general law.[83]

The faithful present at a Mass celebrated in virtue of this privilege, either by a Bishop or by a priest in the Bishop's presence, fulfill the Mass precept for Sundays and Holydays.[84] A reason mentioned for this conclusion is that the general law does not positively exclude the fulfilling of the precept by assisting at Mass offered on a portable altar.[85] But in the case of Bishops, the matter has been authoritatively defined. The Sacred Congregation of Rites on June 8, 1896, stated that the Mass precept was satisfied when

---

[79] Canons 349, § 1, 1° and 239, § 1, 7°.

[80] C. 12, *De Privilegiis,* V, 7, in VI°: ". . . indulgemus eisdem ut altare possint habere viaticum, et in eo celebrare ac facere celebrari. . . ."

[81] Canon 239, § 1, 1°; Coronata, *De Locis et Temporibus Sacris,* n. 125.

[82] Blat, *Commentarium,* II, 208; Vermeersch-Creusen, *Epitome,* I, n. 352; Toso, *Commentaria,* Lib. II, tom. II, p. 39; Bliley, *Altars,* p. 113.

[83] Canon 67; Van Hove, *De Privilegiis,* n. 178.

[84] Cocchi, *Commentarium in Codicem Iuris Canonici ad Usum Scholarum* (8 vols. in 5, Taurini, Romae: Vol. V, 4. ed., 1942), V, pars II, n. 81 (hereafter cited *Commentarium*); Cappello, *De Sacramentis,* I, n. 718, 5; Badii, *Institutiones Iuris Canonici* (2 vols., Vol. I, 3. ed., 1921, Vol. II, 3. ed., 1922, Florentiae), II, n. 359 (hereafter cited *Institutiones*); De Meester, *Compendium,* II, n. 307; Wernz-Vidal, *Ius Canonicum,* Vol. IV, pars I, n. 512.

[85] Canon 1249; Beste, *Introductio in Codicem* (2. ed., Collegeville, Minn.: St. John's Abbey Press, 1944), p. 607 (hereafter cited *Introductio*); Coronata, *Institutiones,* II, n. 824.

one assisted at a Mass celebrated by a Bishop in virtue of his portable altar privilege.[86]

Cappello[87] and Coronata[88] both hold that this reply is still in force. They give no intrinsic reason, but they cite Gasparri (1852-1934) as their authority.[89] Vermeersch-Creusen[90] apparently consider the mentioned decree to be still in force, for they use it as their authority in support of the statement that the Mass precept is satisfied when one assists at a Mass celebrated on a portable altar by a Bishop. Blat[91] claims that it is in virtue of canon 4 that the faithful fulfill the Mass precept under these circumstances. He reasons that it is a right that has been acquired and not expressly revoked by the Code, and hence is still in force.

From this it seems clear that the Mass precept is fulfilled when one assists at a Mass celebrated in virtue of this privilege, at least as it is enjoyed by Bishops and the priests who celebrate in the presence of the Bishops.

It should also be noted that all the faithful who assist at such a Mass may receive Holy Communion.[92]

ARTICE IV. THE PRIVILEGE OF CELEBRATING MASS AT SEA

The privilege of offering the Holy Sacrifice while traveling on the ocean must come from the Holy See. Pope Benedict XIV (1740-1758) enacted this regulation in the Constitution *Aestas* (Oct. 11, 1757).[93] However, before this Constitution was issued, there seemed to be no reason why Bishops could not have celebrated aboard ship in virtue of their portable altar privilege. The original grant of the portable altar by Pope Boniface VIII did not specifically exclude its use on ship-board.[94]

But, actually, the problem of the celebration of Mass aboard

---

[86] *Decr. Auth.*, n. 3903.
[87] *De Sacramentis,* I, n. 718, 16.
[88] *De Locis et Temporibus Sacris,* n. 124, p. 126.
[89] *De Eucharistia,* I, n. 327.
[90] *Epitome,* II, n. 563.
[91] *Commentarium,* II, n. 374.
[92] Canon 869.
[93] N. XXIII—*Fontes,* n. 445.
[94] Cf. *supra,* p. 16, footnote 35.

ship did not arise until rather recent times, for in the early history of sea travel it was customary to make a landing every night, and consequently Bishops who were traveling by water could very easily have erected a portable altar on shore for the celebration of Mass the following morning. Such was the usual practice, as can be inferred from the discussions centering about the possibility of the fulfillment of their obligation by sailors through assisting at Mass offered on shore at a portable altar.[95]

Cases of the celebration of Mass on board ship are very rare before the discovery of America. It is reported that St. Vulfrannus, Bishop of Sens, who lived in the third century, actually celebrated Mass aboard ship.[96] Another early reference tells of St. Maximianus, Bishop of Syracuse, distributing the Body and Blood of Christ to his shipmates after a rather serious storm had subsided. This reference, however, seems to support the fact that it was the custom to carry the Blessed Sacrament while traveling, rather than the fact that the Bishop celebrated Mass in order to communicate those aboard the ship.[97] Regatillo[98] tells of the surprise of the voyagers on a certain ship when a Cardinal Legate while sailing with them ordered Mass to be celebrated aboard the ship. This last incident occurred in 1247.

It is difficult to establish the authenticity of the incidents listed. However, it is certain that with the discovery of America and the increase of long sea voyages in the fifteenth century, some Bishops were lenient in allowing Mass to be celebrated on ships that were making such long voyages.[99] From this fact it appears warranted to infer that these Bishops would themselves have celebrated Mass aboard ship, had they chanced to make similar voyages. For their portable altar privilege was not specifically limited in this regard until the publication of the Constitution *Aestas* of Pope Benedict XIV,[100] even though the Sacred Congregation for the Propa-

---

[95] Gattico, *De Oratoriis,* p. 414.

[96] Bollandus, *Acta Sanctorum* (Martii Tomus Tertius, Parisiis et Romae: apud Victorem Palmè Bibliopolam, 1865), p. 148.

[97] Gattico, *De Oratoriis,* p. 422.

[98] *Ius Sacramentarium,* I, n. 218.

[99] Gattico, *De Oratoriis,* p. 416.

[100] 11 oct. 1757—*Fontes,* n. 445.

gation of the Faith had issued earlier replies on the question of celebrating Mass at sea.[101] Replies of the Sacred Congregations subsequent to the Constitution *Aestas* continually insisted on the provision of that Constitution, which legislated that the privilege of a portable altar did not include the faculty of celebrating Mass at sea.[102]

In the present law the faculty of celebrating Mass at sea is granted by law or indult. Priests who wish to celebrate while making a sea voyage must have a special indult that may be obtained from the Apostolic Delegate, even though they enjoy the privilege of a portable altar.[103] However, neither the Ordinary of the one seeking the indult nor the Ordinary of the port of departure may grant the indult.[104] On the other hand, through a privilege of the general law,[105] new with the Code,[106] Bishops may offer the Holy Sacrifice while making sea voyages. In using this privilege Bishops must observe the necessary precautions,[107] which require that the sea be calm, that there be no danger of profanation, such as the spilling of the Precious Blood, and that another priest be present to hold the chalice should the sea grow rough after the Mass has been started.[108] However, it is no longer absolutely necessary that the Bishop have an assistant priest when celebrating on shipboard.[109] But the other precautions must be observed as they are insisted on whenever the indult is granted.

Aboard the ship the Bishop may celebrate in any place that will not detract from the reverence that should surround the Holy

---

[101] E.g., 20 ian. 1667—*Fontes,* n. 4475.

[102] E.g., S.R.C., *Vincen.,* 4 mart. 1901—*Fontes,* n. 6390; S.C. de Prop. Fide., 13 aug. 1902—*Collectanea S. Congregationis de Propaganda Fide* (2 vols., Romae: Typographia Polyglotta S.C. de Propaganda Fide, 1907), n. 2130 (hereafter cited *Collectanea*).

[103] Faculties of the Apostolic Delegate, cap. IV, n. 37—cf. Beste, *Introductio,* p. 984; canon 822, § 3.

[104] S.R.C., *Vincen.,* 4 mart. 1901—*Fontes,* n. 6390.

[105] Canons 349, § 1, 1°, and 239, § 1, 8°.

[106] Coronata, *De Locis et Temporibus Sacris,* n. 124.

[107] Canon 239, § 1, 8°; "Celebrandi in mari debitis cautelis adhibitis."

[108] S.C. de Prop. Fide, 20 ian. 1667—*Fontes,* n. 4475.

[109] S.R.C., 30 iun. 1908—*Decr. Auth.,* n. 4221; Vermeersch-Creusen, *Epitome,* II, n. 101; Beste, *Introductio,* p. 235.

Sacrifice. His stateroom may be used, provided that it is not so small as to become an unbecoming place for Mass.[110] However, he may not delegate another priest to celebrate in his presence while making such a trip, for the right to do this is joined with the Bishop's privilege of a portable altar,[111] the use of which as such is forbidden at sea.[112] Thus in virtue of this privilege, the Bishop alone may celebrate Mass while making an ocean voyage. If he should wish another priest to celebrate for him, that priest would need an apostolic indult to do so.[113]

This privilege extends to Bishops not only the faculty of celebrating while on an ocean voyage, but also the faculty of celebrating while on lake or river cruises. This extension is based on a reply of the Sacred Congregation for the Propagation of the Faith, which interpreted the term "ocean voyage" (*maritimum iter*), as used in canon 883, as including voyages on lakes and rivers,[114] and the faculty of the Apostolic Delegate by which he may grant priests the faculty of celebrating while voyaging by sea or over streams.[115] The Episcopal privilege of celebrating Mass at sea, then, allows a Bishop to offer the Holy Sacrifice in any decent and respectable place aboard ship, whether the ship be plying the ocean, a lake, or a river.[116]

ARTICLE V. THE PRIVILEGE OF USING THEIR OWN ORDO

The ordo is a calendar according to which the various proper Masses are assigned to the days of the year. The principal ordo is the diocesan ordo, made up from the calendar of the Universal Church,[117] with the addition of the local feasts of the dedication

---

[110] S.C. de Prop. Fide., 13 aug. 1902—*Collectanea*, n. 2130; Coronata, *De Locis et Temporibus Sacris*, p. 78, *nota* 1.

[111] Canons 349, § 1, 1° and 239, § 1, 7°.

[112] Canon 822, § 3.

[113] Benedictus XIV, const. *Aestas*, 11 oct. 1757, n. XXIII—*Fontes*, n. 445; Coronata, *loc. cit.*

[114] S.C. de Prop. Fide., 27 iun. 1914—Bouscaren, *Digest*, II, 219.

[115] Faculties of the Apostolic Delegate, cap. IV, n. 37—cf. Beste, *Introductio*, p. 984.

[116] Hynes, *The Privileges of Cardinals*, p. 75.

[117] This calendar is found in the beginning of the Roman Missal and the Roman Breviary.

of the cathedral, the titular Saint of the cathedral, the dedication of all consecrated churches in the diocese, the feasts of the principal and secondary patrons of the diocese, the province, and the nation, as well as the feasts of local saints approved by the Holy See. Regular Orders approved by the Holy See also have a proper ordo, which is to be followed in the churches and oratories subject to them. With this exception, then, Mass is to be offered according to the ordo of the diocese in which it is celebrated.[118]

The general law specifying the ordo to be followed in the celebration of Mass in a church or public oratory has been determined by the Sacred Congregation of Rites. Each and every priest, secular or Regular, is required to celebrate the Mass, even if it be proper to the religious, according to the calendar of the church in which he celebrates, to the exclusion, however, of the rites peculiar to the respective church or religious institute.[119]

An exception to this general regulation in virtue of a privilege allows all Bishops to celebrate in all places according to their own ordo.[120] The ordo is usually derived from the diocese to which the celebrant is attached.[121] Residential and coadjutor Bishops, as well as Apostolic Administrators who are Bishops, clearly have a proper ordo, as they are assigned to a definite diocese, whose ordo then is their proper ordo. Purely titular Bishops who are, in a way, without a diocese, such as retired Bishops, since they are entitled to the use of a privilege granted to them,[122] would be safe in adopting as their own ordo the ordo of the diocese in which they have a residence. The Apostolic Delegate in virtue of his faculties obtains a proper ordo. He may celebrate Mass according to the Roman Calendar.[123]

---

[118] O'Connell, *The Celebration of Mass,* I, 57.

[119] S.R.C., *Urbis et Orbis,* 9 iul. 1895—*Decr. Auth.,* n. 3826; S.R.C., *Ruthenen.,* 22 maii 1896—*Decr. Auth.,* n. 3910; *Missale Romanum,* additiones et variationes in Rubricis Missalis, tit. IV, n. 6; Wuest, *Matters Liturgical* (translated and revised by Thos. Mullaney, New York: Fr. Pustet Co., 6. ed., 1942), n. 353; Vermeersch-Creusen, *Epitome,* II, n. 92.

[120] Canons 349, § 1, 1° and 239, § 1, 9°.

[121] O'Connell, *The Celebration of Mass,* I, 58.

[122] Canon 68.

[123] Faculties of the Apostolic Delegate, cap. VI, n. 51—Beste, *Introductio,* p. 685.

The privilege of using their own ordo entitles Bishops to celebrate Mass according to the ordo of their diocese in a church or oratory of another diocese or of a religious institute having an ordo of its own, even though the latter differ from the calendar of the place wherein the Holy Sacrifice is offered. This would extend also to the permissible offering of a votive Mass allowed by the Bishop's ordo.

ARTICLE VI. THE PRIVILEGE OF ENJOYING DAILY THE FACULTY OF A PERSONALLY PRIVILEGED ALTAR

In addition to the other privileges which center about the Sacrifice of the Mass, Bishops enjoy the faculty of a personally privileged altar every day on which they offer Mass for a departed soul.[124]

A privileged altar is so called for the reason that the Mass celebrated at such an altar is enriched with a plenary indulgence applicable to the soul in purgatory for whom the Mass is offered.[125] If measured by the mind of the Holy Father and the use of the power of the keys, its efficacy is such that it would deliver a soul from purgatory at once; but if the actual effect of the Mass be considered, the indulgence is to be measured in so far as it is acceptable to the Divine Mercy.[126] The purpose of the Church in applying this indulgence is to liberate a determined soul from the sufferings of purgatory. But whether or not this purpose will be fully achieved depends entirely upon the acceptance of the indulgence by Almighty God, who is in no way bound to accept such a payment for the debt of sin.[127]

The privileged altar may be either a real or a personal privilege. When the privilege is attached to an altar it is a real privilege,

---

[124] Canons 349, § 1, 1° and 239, § 1, 10°.

[125] Blat, *Commentarium,* lib. III, pars I, p. 307; De Angelis, *De Indulgentiis, Tractatus Quoad Earum Naturam et Usum* (Colle Don Bosco [Asti]: Libreria Dottrina Cristiana, 1946), n. 302 (hereafter cited *De Indulgentiis*).

[126] S.C. Indulg., *Sancti Flori,* 28 iul. 1840—*Decreta Authentica Sacrae Congregationis Indulgentiis Sacrisque Reliquiis Praepositae* (Ratisbonae, 1883), n. 283 (hereafter cited *Decr. Auth. S.C. Indulg.*).

[127] Augustine, *A Commentary on the New Code of Canon Law* (8 vols., St. Louis: B. Herder Book Co.; Vol. I, 1918; Vols. II, III, V, 1919; Vol. IV, 1920; Vol. VI, 1921; Vol. VII, 1923; Vol. VIII, 1922), IV, 366 (hereafter cited *Commentary*).

and everyone who celebrates at such an altar enjoys the privilege.[128] When the privilege is granted directly to an individual priest wherever he celebrates Mass, it is a personal privilege, and makes the altar at which such a priest celebrates a privileged altar for that Mass.[129]

Bishops daily enjoy the use of the privileged altar as a personal privilege, so that wherever or whenever they celebrate, whether on a portable or on a fixed altar, the altar becomes privileged, provided that the Mass be offered for a departed soul,[130] and to the fruits of the Mass thus offered there is added a plenary indulgence granted to the soul in purgatory *per modum suffragii.*[131]

In order to apply the indulgence of the privileged altar to a departed soul the Bishop must offer the Holy Sacrifice for that soul, as the application of the Mass and the application of the indulgence are not to be separated.[132] However, if he offers Mass for several or all of the faithful departed, he should determine upon the soul to whom the plenary indulgence is to be applied, as the general law does not allow for the division of the indulgence among many souls.[133] Should he neglect this determination before celebrating the Mass, the indulgence is not rendered useless, as its application is then left to the Will of God who well knows to whom it should be applied.[134]

---

[128] Coronata, *Institutiones,* I, n. 87; Bliley, *Altars,* p. 123.

[129] De Meester, *Compendium,* III, n. 1159; Coronata, *De Sacramentis,* I, n. 487; De Angelis, *De Indulgentiis,* n. 306.

[130] S.C. Indulg., *Mechlinien.,* 20 mart. 1846, ad 2—*Decr. Auth. S.C. Indulg.,* n. 334; 15 mart. 1852—*Decr. Auth. S.C. Indulg.,* n. 351.

[131] When the plenary indulgence is applied *per modum suffragii,* the Church offers to God an indulgence gained by the living, and in doing so it offers the remission of the debt if God will be pleased to accept it, together with the Church's own most efficacious intercession—Davis, *Moral,* III, 416; De Angelis, *De Indulgentiis,* n. 13.

[132] S.C. Indulg., 5 aug. 1897—*Acta Sanctae Sedis* (Romae, 1865-1908), XXX (1897-1898), 278 (hereafter cited *ASS*). On special occasion, such as the jubilee year, the Holy Father has allowed the application of the indulgence of the privileged altar independently of the application of the Mass.—S. Poenit., 10 iun. 1942—*AAS,* XXXIV (1942), 210; Bouscaren, *Digest,* II, 223.

[133] S.C. Indulg., *Viennen.,* 18 dec. 1885—*ASS,* XVII (1885), 341.

[134] S.C. Indulg., *Veronen.,* 12 mart. 1885, ad I—*Decr. Auth. S.C. Indulg.,* n. 366; S.C.S. Off. (Sect. de Indulg.), 17 iun. 1915—*AAS,* VII (1915), 410.

Thus it is clear that the Bishop need not advert to his privilege of the privileged altar. For if he offers Mass for a departed soul, the plenary indulgence would be automatically (*ipso facto*) applied to that soul.[134a] The reason for this statement rests on the fact that the Bishop does not gain the indulgence in question. He but places the act, the celebration of Mass, by force of which the indulgence is applied by the Church to the soul for whom the Mass is offered.[135] In view of these regulations it is clear that a Bishop may not apply the indulgence of the privileged altar when he is offering Mass for the living. Nor may he apply it when he offers the same Mass for both the living and the dead, as the application of the Mass and the indulgence may not be separated.[136]

It is at least the common opinion[137] that the celebrant need not be in the state of grace to obtain the indulgence of the privileged altar. However, Cappello[138] maintains along with De Angelis[139] and Fanfani[140] that it is certain that the celebrant need not be in the state of grace in order to obtain the indulgence attached to a privileged altar. For the efficacy of the privilege does not depend, they say, on the personal dispositions of the celebrant, but entirely upon the free grant of the Church. Cappello and Fanfani gave a reply of the Sacred Congregation of Indulgences[141] as authority for their position.

The former liturgical requirements of Mass in black vestments, and the inclusion of the *oratio pro defunctis* in the Mass of the

---

[134a] S.C. Indulg., *Romana*, 19 iun. 1880—*Decr. Auth. S.C. Indulg.*, n. 451.

[135] De Angelis, *De Indulgentiis*, n. 304.

[136] S.C. Indulg., 5 aug. 1897—*ASS*, XXX (1897-1898), 278; Cappello, *De Sacramentis*, I, n. 719; Melata, "An Missa et Indulgentia Altaris Privilegiati Reparari Possint"—*Analecta Ecclesiastica* (Romae, 1893-1911), III (1895), 83-86; Bliley, *Altars*, p. 125.

[137] Wernz-Vidal, *Ius Canonicum*, Vol. VI, pars I, n. 161, *nota* 62; Regatillo, *Ius Sacramentarium*, I, n. 703; Coronata, *De Sacramentis*, I, n. 489, p. 535.

[138] *De Sacramentis*, I, n. 719, p. 680; II, n. 644.

[139] *De Indulgentiis*, n. 320.

[140] *De Indulgentiis* (2. ed., notabiliter aucta, Romae; Marietti: 1926), n. 102 (hereafter cited *De Indulgentiis*).

[141] 12 mart. 1855—*Decr. Auth. S.C. Indulg.*, n. 366.

day whenever possible,[142] are no longer necessary for the gaining of the indulgence. Today the indulgence may be gained by the Bishop no matter what Mass he offers, either a requiem Mass or the Mass of the feast or of the Vigil.[143]

ARTICLE VII. THE PRIVILEGED STATUS OF THE EPISCOPAL ORATORY

The chapel or oratory which the Bishop has in his residence, even though it be private, enjoys all the rights and privileges of a semi-public oratory.[144] This recognition of the private nature of the Episcopal oratory is new with the Code. But these rights and privileges were granted to the Bishop's chapel before the Code. In 1751, Pope Benedict XIV (1740-1758)[145] declared the homes of Bishops to have the juridic standing of a public place. The purpose of this declaration was twofold; first, to show that the Bishop's oratory, even though in his own residence, was not comprehended under the prohibition of the Council of Trent which forbade the celebration of Mass in a private house;[146] and secondly, to show that the faithful in attending Mass in these oratories fulfilled the Mass precept. Previous to this, however, the Sacred Congregations had issued like regulations.[147]

Pope Benedict XIV in establishing the public status of the Episcopal residence determined beyond a doubt that the oratories therein enjoyed the rights just mentioned. Such action was probably occasioned by the fact that the semi-public oratory in which the Mass precept could likewise be fulfilled was not officially established until 1899.[148]

The establishment of the semi-public oratory does not seem to

---

[142] S.C. Indulg., 2 apr. 1840, ad 2 et 3—*Decr. Auth. S.C. Indulg.*, n. 339; S.R.C., 12 iun. 1912—*AAS*, IV (1912), 446.

[143] S.C.S. Off. (Sect. de Indulg.), 20 febr. 1913—*AAS*, V (1913), 122.

[144] Canon 1189.

[145] Ep. encycl. "Magno cum," 2 iul. 1751, ad 2—*Fontes*, n. 413.

[146] Sess. XXII, *de Sacrificio Missae*, c. 9, *de observandis et evitandis in celebratione missae*—Schroeder, *Council of Trent*, p. 423.

[147] S.C.C., 18 febr. 1623—*Fontes*, n. 2436; S.R.C., *Bituntina*, 2 iul. 1661—*Decr. Auth.*, n. 1196.

[148] S.R.C., decr. 23 ian. 1899—*Fontes*, n. 6288; Ayrinhac, *Administrative Legislation in the New Code of Canon Law* (New York: Longmans, Green & Co., 1930), p. 41 (hereafter cited *Administrative Legislation*).

have changed the public status of the Episcopal residence. The Code allows for the oratory to be private, but confers on the Episcopal oratory by privilege all the rights and privileges of the semi-public oratory.[149] Thus even the private oratory of the Bishop enjoys today all the rights and privileges which Pope Benedict XIV obtained for it by declaring it in fact a public oratory. This is clear from a study of the canons dealing with oratories. In a semi-public oratory all divine offices and ecclesiastical functions may be celebrated which the local ordinary permits.[150] These functions are substantially the same as those which may be held in a public oratory, as is supported by a comparison of canon 1191, § 2, with canon 1193.[151] Hence the privileges and rights of the Episcopal oratory are substantially the same in the Code as they were previously, even though the Code provides for the existence of a private episcopal chapel or oratory.

Specifically, in virtue of canon 1189, any number of Masses may be celebrated in an Episcopal oratory. The priests who celebrate Mass therein require no special delegation, and further the presence of the Bishop at the Mass is not required, as such celebration may continue in the Episcopal oratory even during the vacancy of the diocesan see.[152] The faithful who attend these Masses not only fulfill their obligation,[153] but they may also receive Holy Communion.[154]

Marriages may be celebrated in these oratories, provided that the necessary permission be obtained. Canon 1109, § 1, requires that permission be obtained from the local Ordinary or local pastor to celebrate a marriage in a semi-public oratory. This permission must be obtained by all titular Bishops, who have not a status equal to that of a Bishop Ordinary, before they may celebrate a marriage in their own chapel.[155]

---

[149] Canon 1189.

[150] Canon 1193.

[151] Coronata, *Institutiones,* II, n. 767.

[152] S.R.C., *Bosanen.,* 8 apr. 1854—*Decr. Auth.,* n. 5200; Gasparri, *De Eucharistia,* I, n. 229; De Meester, *Compendium,* III, n. 1150.

[153] S.R.C., *Urbis et Orbis,* 8 iun. 1896—*Decr. Auth.,* n. 3906; canon 1249.

[154] Canon 896.

[155] A titular Bishop who is a Vicar General could celebrate a marriage in his chapel, as he in virtue of canon 198, § 1, is considered a local Ordinary,

It is likewise necessary that proper delegation be obtained for the marriage in accordance with canons 1095 and 1096. Bishops Ordinary, however, since they may validly assist at marriage and may grant permission for their celebration in a semi-public oratory, can assist at marriages in their own chapels without obtaining permission or delegation. As for the other sacraments, all functions proper to the Bishop, such as Confirmation and Ordinations, may be held in the Bishop's chapel,[156] though, as De Meester[157] points out, it would not be fitting to hold such functions there with regularity. Likewise candles, palms, etc., may be solemnly blessed and distributed in these chapels.[158]

Bishops do not have the privilege of reserving the Blessed Sacrament in their oratories. To do so they would need an apostolic indult.[159] However, if a community of sisters care for the Episcopal residence and make use of the oratory therein, Bishops Ordinary can then reserve the Blessed Sacrament in their chapel. Coronata[160] claims that authors recognize the existence of the Bishop's right to reserve the Blessed Sacrament even in their private oratory. The authors cited are Augustine[161] and Vermeersch-Creusen in an earlier edition.[162]

In the sixth edition, Vermeersch-Creusen[163] mentions that, even though in former editions they followed Augustine in holding that the Blessed Sacrament could be reserved in the Episcopal oratory without an apostolic indult, they no longer hold this position. In the sixth edition they teach that Bishops do not enjoy the privilege of reserving the Blessed Sacrament in their oratories for the following reasons. The privileges of a semi-public oratory as such do not include the privilege of reserving the Blessed Sacrament. The reservation of the Blessed Sacrament may be had in these oratories

---

and thus capable of granting permission for such a celebration of marriage according to canon 1109, § 1.

156 Canons 791 and 1009, § 2.

157 *Compendium,* III, n. 1150.

158 Canons 1189 and 1193; Cappello, *Summa,* II, n. 437.

159 Canon 1265, § 2.

160 *Institutiones,* II, n. 844.

161 *Commentary,* VI, 218.

162 *Epitome* (vol. II, 2. ed., 1926), n. 589.

163 *Epitome,* II, n. 589.

when such oratories serve as the principal oratory of pious or religious houses. The episcopal residence does not constitute, in a technical sense, either a pious or a religious house. Furthermore, the practice in Rome does not favor the extension to the episcopal chapel of the permission mentioned in canon 1264, § 1, 2°, whereby the Blessed Sacrament may be reserved in a semi-public oratory that serves as the principal oratory of a pious or a religious house. Following the latter opinion of Vermeersch-Creusen together with Bouscaren-Ellis,[164] the writer maintains that Bishops may not reserve the Blessed Sacrament in their chapels without an apostolic indult.

However, should a community of sisters care for the episcopal residence and use the chapel therein as the customary place in which they attend to their religious duties, the Bishop Ordinary can allow the Blessed Sacrament to be reserved for them in his chapel. The reason for this position is as follows. A community of at least three sisters would constitute the collegiate moral person necessary for the establishment of a religious house,[165] which does not demand the existence of a separate physical building for its establishment.[166] Hence, if the sisters caring for the domestic needs of the Episcopal residence use the Bishop's chapel as the usual oratory in which they attend to their religious duties, the law allows the Bishop Ordinary to reserve the Blessed Sacrament for them in his chapel.[167] In the same circumstances the Blessed Sacrament may be reserved in the chapel of a titular Bishop, provided that the local Ordinary gives the necessary permission.[168]

Bishops are not obliged to seek the permission of the local Ordinary in establishing their oratories. For these chapels, though enjoying the rights and privileges of the semi-public oratory, are not

---

[164] *Canon Law, Text and Commentary* (Milwaukee: Bruce Publishing Co., 1946), p. 645 (hereafter cited Bouscaren-Ellis, *Canon Law*).

[165] Canons 100, § 2, and 488, 5°; Cappello, *Summa*, II, n. 4; Coronata, *Institutiones*, I, n. 504; Wernz-Vidal, *Ius Canonicum*, Vol. IV, pars I, n. 477, p. 538, *nota* 20.

[166] Pontificia Commissio ad Codicis Canones authentice Interpretandos (hereafter cited PCI), 2 iunii 1918, ad V—*AAS*, X (1918), 346.

[167] Canon 1265, § 1, 2°; Cappello, *De Sacramentis*, I, n. 320, 2°, 3°; Coronata, *Institutiones*, II, n. 844, p. 165.

[168] Canon 1265, § 1, 2°.

subject to the regulations affecting the latter.[170] Hence, Bishops may erect their own private oratories[171] and celebrate Mass therein without obtaining permission or being subject to a preliminary visitation, as is required by the Code for semi-public and private oratories.[172] Further, the number of oratories is not limited to one in the Episcopal residence proper. Bishops may establish chapels having all the rights and privileges of semi-public oratories in every house either in or outside of their diocese, provided that they retain these houses for the purpose of residence.[173]

In all these chapels, since they are similar by privilege to semi-public oratories, Bishops may have consecrated fixed altars.[174]

ARTICLE VIII. THE LITURGICAL PRIVILEGES ENJOYED BY BISHOPS IN THE CELEBRATION OF MASS

By way of privilege all Bishops, both residential and titular, may wear a ring, a zucchetto or skull-cap,[175] and be assisted by a priest while offering the Holy Sacrifice.[176]

The origin of these practices is difficult to determine. As early as 633 the IV Council of Toledo in Spain spoke of the ring as the sign of the Episcopal office.[177] By the year 1000, however, the use of the Episcopal ring was practically universal. Still it seems that the wearing of it during the celebration of Mass was forbidden.[178]

The IV General Council of the Lateran (1215) allowed the use of a ring, provided that its use was in keeping with the official

---

[170] Canon 1189; Coronata, *De Locis et Temporibus Sacris*, n. 94, 3.

[171] Vermeersch-Creusen, *Epitome*, II, n. 502.

[172] Canons 1192, §§ 1, 2, and 1195, § 1; Coronata, *Institutiones*, II, n. 722.

[173] Gasparri, *De Eucharistia*, I, n. 288; Many, *Praelectiones Canonicae de Locis Sacris* (Parisiis, 1904), n. 100 (hereafter cited *De Locis Sacris*); Chelodi, *Ius de Personis*, n. 195; Cappello, *Summa*, I, n. 388.

[174] Bliley, *Altars*, p. 77.

[175] Canon 811, § 2.

[176] Canon 812.

[177] Mansi, *Sacrorum Conciliorum Nova et Amplissima Collectio* (53 vols. in 60, Parisiis, 1901-1927), X, 624 (hereafter cited Mansi).

[178] Augustine, *Liturgical Law, A Handbook of the Roman Liturgy* (St. Louis and London: B. Herder Book Co., 1931), p. 60.

dignity of the person wearing it.[179] Though this legislation certainly supports the fact that a Bishop could wear a ring, it does not indicate necessarily that a Bishop could wear a ring while celebrating Mass. However, the Council may have had reference to such a practice, since the Pontifical of Durant's (1238-1296) published about 1284,[180] spoke of the assistant priest's duty of removing and replacing the Bishop's ring during a pontifical Mass, as though it were a practice of long standing.[181] Thus it seems practically certain that in the year 1284 Bishops were wearing a ring while celebrating pontifical Mass.[182]

The *Bishop's Ceremonial*[183] and the *Roman Pontifical*[184] imply that the Bishop should have at least two rings, the pontifical ring for use in pontifical Mass, and the gemmed or ordinary ring. Today's custom favors the use of one ring, the ordinary ring adorned with a simple gem or large stone surrounded by brilliants.[185] The stone may be of any type except sapphire, which is reserved for

---

[179] Can. 16, ". . . fibulos omnino non ferant neque corrigas auri vel argenti ornatum habentes, sed nec annulos, nisi quibus competit et officio dignitatis . . . " (c. 15, X, *de vita et honestate clericorum,* III, 1) ; Schroeder, *Disciplinary Decrees of the General Councils* (Text, Translation and Commentary, St. Louis and London: Herder Book Co., 1937), p. 569 (hereafter cited *Disciplinary Decrees*) ; Mansi, XII, 1006.

[180] This Pontifical aimed at giving a complete list of Episcopal ceremonies by dispensing with those not used by a Bishop. At the time of Pope Clement V (1305-1314) it was considered the best pontifical available. Though this pontifical may never have been officially adopted, it served as a basis for all later authentic pontificals.—Callewaert, *Liturgicae Institutiones, Tractatus Primus de S.Liturgia Universim* (2. ed., Brugis: Apud Carolum Beyaert, Editorem Pontificum, 1925), n. 94.

[181] Durandus, *Rationale Divinorum Officiorum* (accedit aliud Divinorum Officiorum Rationale a Joanne Bellethro, Naples, 1895), pp. 219 et seq (hereafter cited *Rationale Officiorum*).

[182] Catalanus, *Caeremoniale Episcoporum,* II, 94.

[183] *Caeremoniale Episcoporum,* Lib. II, cap. VIII, n. 10.

[184] *Pontificale Romanum Summorum Pontificum jussu editum a Benedicto XIV et Leone XIII Pont. Max. recognitum et castigatum, ed. secunda* (New York, Fr. Pustet & Co., 1908), Lib. I, *de ordine conferendis,* cap. III, art. IV.

[185] Nainfa, *Costume of Prelates of the Catholic Church* (new and revised edition, Baltimore: John Murphy Co., 1926), pp. 139, 140 (hereafter cited *Costume of Prelates*).

Cardinals.[186] It is this ordinary ring which is now used in the celebration of Mass.

Though the Bishop in administering Holy Communion is free to present or not to present the ring to the recipient,[187] the faithful may obtain an indulgence of fifty days by kissing the ring when it is offered.[188] Furthermore, the faithful in kissing the Bishop's ring should go on their knee to a Bishop in his own diocese, to an Archbishop in his own province, to the Apostolic Delegate in the entire country. In all other cases the faithful should bow before kissing the ring as a mark of respect for the Episcopate.[189]

The ring, since it partakes of a strictly pontifical nature, may not be used by a priest who has received official notification of his promotion to the Episcopate. It may be worn only after consecration has been received.[190]

It is, as in the case of the Episcopal ring, equally difficult to determine when Bishops began to wear the zucchetto during the Holy Sacrifice. In the eighth century the practice of wearing some type of head dress at Mass must have been rather common in Rome, as Pope Zachary (741-751) in a Roman Synod of 743 forbade Bishops and clerics to assist at Mass with their heads covered.[191] This, of course, does not necessarily imply that the celebrant of the Mass was also using a head dress. But by the middle of the twelfth century Bishops were probably using the zucchetto at Mass. *The Bishops' Ceremonial*[192] requires the wearing of the zucchetto to prevent the miter from being soiled. The miter itself appeared as a mark of the Episcopate around 1150.[193] From this fact it

---

[186] Nainfa, *Costume of Prelates,* p. 142.

[187] S.R.C., 8 maii 1925—*AAS,* XVII (1925), 265.

[188] S.C.S. Off. (Sect. de Indulg.), 18 mart. 1909—*AAS,* I (1909), 277.

[189] Nainfa, *Costume of Prelates,* p. 144.

[190] Cappello, *Summa,* I, n. 387; Toso, *Commentaria,* Lib. II, p. 180; Regatillo, *Institutiones Iuris Canonici* (2 vols., Santander: Sal Terrae; Vol. I, 1941; Vol. II, 1942), I, n. 496, p. 245 (hereafter cited *Institutiones*).

[191] C. 57, D. I, *de cons.;* Canons 13 and 14 of the Synod—Mansi, XII, 365.

[192] *Caeremoniale Episcoporum,* Lib. I, cap. VIII, n. 37.

[193] The bronze doors of the Cathedral of Benevento, wrought about 1150, represent the Archbishop of that city with his twenty suffragan Bishops all wearing the miter.—Nainfa, *Costume of Prelates,* pp. 145, 146.

seems warranted to conclude that the zucchetto was introduced at this time for the purpose mentioned in the present ceremonials.[194]

In the year 1867, Pope Pius IX (1846-1878) granted to Bishops the privilege of wearing a purple zucchetto as an exclusive sign of Episcopal dignity.[195]

The use of this purple zucchetto extends not only to the celebration of Mass but to all ecclesiastical functions. During Mass the zucchetto is worn at all times except from the Sanctus till the last ablutions.[196] While assisting at Mass when vested in a cope, the Bishop wears the zucchetto except at the consecration and elevation.[197] While assisting at Mass in choir habit (cappa magna, mozzetta or mantelletta) the Bishop removes the zucchetto during the reading of the gospel and when he receives incensation,[198] as well as during the consecration and elevation. But in the presence of the Blessed Sacrament exposed, the zucchetto is not worn, and Bishops are further advised to remove it when engaged in some external act of private devotion such as genuflecting, or kissing the relic of a Saint.[199]

The zucchetto, unlike the ring, may be worn by a priest from the moment he receives official notification of his advancement to the Episcopate.[200]

The Bishop's privilege of enjoying the assistance of a priest in offering the Holy Sacrifice is thought to have had its origin in the ancient custom of concelebration, by which the Bishop and his priests offered together the same sacrifice.[201] But whether or not

[194] Nainfa, *loc. cit.*

[195] Brev. *Ecclesiarum omnium,* 17 iun. 1867—*ASS,* III (1867), 158.

[196] S.C. Consist., 2 maii 1910—*AAS,* II (1910), 330.

[197] S.R.C., *Oppiden.*, 14 iun. 1845, ad 3 et 4.—*Decr. Auth.*, n. 2895.

[198] S.R.C., *Montes Regalis,* 10 maii 1890—*Decr. Auth.*, n. 3728.

[199] De Herdt, *Praxis Pontificalis seu Caeremonialis Episcoporum Practica Expositio* (3 vols., 2. ed., Lovanii, 1906), I, 31 (hereafter cited *Praxis Pontificalis*); Nainfa, *Costume of Prelates,* p. 117.

[200] S.C. Consist., 2 maii 1910—*AAS,* II (1910), 330.

[201] Catalanus, *Pontificale Romanum in Tres Partes Distributum Clementis VIII ac Urbani VIII Auctoritate, nunc primum prolegomenis et Commentariis Illustratum* (3 vols., Parisiis, 1852), I, 20 (hereafter cited *Pontificale Romanum*); Woywod, *A Practical Commentary on the Code of Canon Law* (2 vols., 10th printing, revised by Callistus Smith, New York; Joseph F. Wagner, 1946), I, 372 (hereafter cited *Commentary*).

this is the origin of the custom which employs the aid of an assistant priest, the custom is rather old. Catalanus[202] cited some ancient ordinals and rituals in which are described the Masses celebrated in Rome and in other cities by Bishops who were assisted by not less than two or more than five priests. However, it is certain that by the eleventh century the office of the assistant priest, as we know it today, was well established. The evidence of this is found in the Pontifical of Durantis.[203]

Today, when a Bishop celebrates a Pontifical Mass, he should be assisted by a priest vested in a *pluviale*.[204] The priest chosen for this office should be either the Vicar-General, or a priest of high rank, or the priest who is to preach the sermon.[205] While celebrating a *Missa cantata* or a *Missa privata* a Bishop may be assisted by a priest vested in surplice.[206] If the custom exists, the priest thus assisting a Bishop may wear a stole either for the entire Mass or from the Consecration to the Communion.[207] The stole is not of obligation. Its use depends on custom so that it is worn only if custom dictates it.

---

[202] *Caeremoniale Episcoporum,* II, 213, sub § 1.
[203] *Rationale Officiorum,* pp. 219 seq.
[204] *Caeremoniale Episcoporum,* lib. I, cap. VII, n. 3.
[205] *Ibid.,* n. 4.
[206] *Op. cit.,* lib. I, cap. XXIX, n. 2.
[207] S.R.C., 15 sept. 1781—*Decr. Auth.,* n. 1520.

CHAPTER III

PRIVILEGES THAT GRANT EXEMPTIONS IN JUDICIAL PROCEDURE AND PENAL LEGISLATION

ARTICLE I. THE GENERAL PRIVILEGE OF EXEMPTION IN THE JUDICIAL FORUM AS ENJOYED BY BISHOPS

The Church as a completely self-contained society has a right to enact a system of laws to aid its members in attaining the end for which the Church was established. The laws themselves are aimed at preserving external order in the relationships existing between the Church and its members, and among the members themselves. As it is natural that these laws will be called into question when controversies arise between the members, or when delinquent members injure the common good of the Church, it is necessary that the Church have a judiciary system which will properly interpret and apply the laws in such situation.

The laws governing this judicial system have been set forth in the Fourth Book of the Code. Therein are determined the solemnities to be followed according to the person, the place or the type of case in litigation.[1] These solemnities indicate which of several forums is competent to hear and give a definite sentence in a specific trial,[2] and it is through them that the Church has established the exemption from the power and the jurisdiction of the secular tribunals which is enjoyed by all clerics, all religious of both sexes, and all members of pious societies who live in common without vows.[3]

This exemption is known as the privilege of the forum. It forbids the bringing of any cleric before a civil tribunal without the permission of his competent superior. This privilege may be considered a specific privilege of the Episcopate in so far as the competent

[1] Solieri, *Institutiones Iuris Ecclesiastici* (2. ed., Romae: Fr. Pustet, 1921), pp. 135-140, 167-169 (hereafter cited *Institutiones*); Beste, *Introductio*, pp. 40, 41.

[2] Cappello, *Summa*, III, n. 9.

[3] Canons 120, § 1; 614; 680.

superior is none less than the Holy See. For a Bishop may not be brought before a civil tribunal without the permission of the Holy See.[4]

The privilege of the forum is of early origin in both civil and ecclesiastical law. Local councils and synods between the years 324 and 615 decreed in general that clerics were not to be brought before a civil judge without the permission or knowledge of their Bishop.[5] This legislation received pontifical approval towards the end of the sixth century in the time of Pope St. Gregory (590-604), as is clear from his letters.[6]

By civil enactment, Emperor Honorius III (395-423) recommended that all clerics be tried before a Bishop.[7] Later, Emperor Justinian (527-565) enacted into law this recommendation by reserving to the Bishop all trials involving clerics, nuns, or ascetics.[8]

Even at this period Bishops enjoyed a more extensive privileged forum than that of ordinary clerics in the provision of both ecclesiastical and civil law. An indication of this is found in the fifth canon of the I General Council of Nicaea (325), in which it was

---

[4] Canon 120, § 2. Patres Cardinales, Legati Sedis Apostolicae, Episcopi etiam titulares, Abbates vel Praelati *nullius,* supremi religionum iuris pontificii Superiores, Officiales maiores Romanae Curiae, ob negotia ad ipsorum munus pertinentia, apud iudicem laicum conveniri nequeunt sine venia Sedis Apostolicae; . . .

[5] E.g., Roman Synod (324), c. 16—Hardouin, *Acta Conciliorum et Epistolae Decretales ac Constitutiones Summorum Pontificum* (12 vols., Parisiis, 1714-1715), I, 293 (hereafter cited Hardouin); Council of Agde in France (circa 506), c. 32—Bruns, *Canones Apostolorum et Conciliorum Saeculorum* IV-VII (2 vols., Berolini, Reimeri, 1839), II, 152 (hereafter cited Bruns); III Council of Orleans (538), c. 32—Mansi, IX, 19; c. 2, C. XI, q. I (c. 2, X, *de foro competenti,* II, 2; V Council of Paris 615, c. 4—Bruns, II, 256).

[6] C. 40, C. XI, q. I (Letter written about 594)—Jaffé, *Regesta Pontificum Romanorum ab condita Ecclesia ad annum post Christum natum MCXCVIII* (2. ed. cura G. Wattenbach, F. Kaltenbrunner, P. Ewald, S. Loewenfeld, 2 vols. in 1, Lipsiae, 1885-1888), n. 1298 (hereafter cited Jaffé); c. 39, C. XI, q. I (Letter to John, Bishop of Syracuse, written about 602)—Jaffé, n. 1812; c. 38, C. XI, q. I (Letter written about 603)—Jaffé, n. 1912.

[7] "Clericos non nisi apud episcopos accusari convenit"—*Codex Theodosianus* (ed. Paulus Krueger, Berolini: Apud Weidmannos, 1928), (16. 2) 41.

[8] *Corpus Iuris Civilis,* Vol. III, *Novellae* (5. ed., recognovit Rudolfus Schoell, absolvit Gulielmus Kroll, Berolini: apud Weidmannos, 1928), *Novellae* (123. 21).

ordered that anyone who wished to contest the justice of a sentence passed by a Bishop had to bring the case before the provincial synod.[9] The ninth canon of the General Council of Chalcedon (451) was more specific in providing that all cases against a Bishop were to be tried before the provincial synod or the metropolitan.[10] Justinian granted Bishops full immunity from the civil tribunals in all judicial cases.[11] The privilege of the forum was observed in accordance with these provisions until the ninth century. Bishops enjoyed full exemption from the jurisdiction of the civil tribunals, while the lesser clerics were tried before the Bishop, though they were punished by the civil authority when found guilty of a criminal offense.[12]

With the advent of the pseudo-Isidorian Decretals (circa 847-852), the privilege of clerical exemption received a major extension. This work, which was aimed at freeing the Church from the evils of lay domination, made use of both authentic and spurious documents to establish a more extensive privileged forum.[13] The influence of this work in the later development of the privileged forum is evident. Gratian listed numerous pseudo-Isidorian documents in support of clerical exemption from the jurisdiction of civil tribunals.[14]

It was at this period that the privileged forum developed into a form most like the present form. From the ninth century forward, all the clergy were exempted from the competence of the civil tribunals in all cases whether civil or criminal, as was formerly the case. But the privilege was more extensive in this that the ecclesiastical tribunals were competent to try a cleric not only on a criminal charge but they were competent also to punish the cleric if he was found guilty.[15]

---

[9] Schroeder, *Disciplinary Decrees,* p. 28.

[10] *Op. cit.,* p. 98.

[11] *Novellae* (123. 22).

[12] *Novellae* (83. 1); Bachofen, *Summa Iuris Ecclesiastici Publici* (New York: Fr. Pustet, 1910), p. 79 (hereafter cited *Summa*).

[13] Van Hove, *Commentarium Lovaniense in Codicem Iuris Canonici,* Vol. I, tom. I, *Prolegomena de Codicem Iuris Canonici* (2. ed., Mechliniae-Romae: H. Dessain, 1945), pp. 306, 307 (hereafter cited *Prolegomena*).

[14] E.g., cc. 2, 5, 6, 7, 8, C. II, q. 6; cc. 1, 3, 9, 10, C. XI, q. 1.

[15] Letter of Pope Nicholas I (858-867) to Salaman, King of the Bretons (c. 10, C. III, q. 6)—Jaffé, n. 2789: Roman Synod (1095), cc. 6, 10.—Mansi, XIX, 898.

The Council of Trent (1545-1563) ruled that a Bishop could not be cited or warned to appear in court except for a cause for which he may be deposed from or deprived of his office.[16]

The need of obtaining the permission of the Holy See before citing a Bishop before a lay judge is found in a reply of the Holy Office dated January 23, 1886.[17] This reply was given as an interpretation of the automatic (*ipso facto*) excommunication, reserved in a special manner to the Holy See, which was attached by Pope Pius IX to the crime of bringing a Bishop into civil court without permission.[18] The excommunication which is in force today, even antedates this Constitution of Pope Pius IX. Pope Martin V (1417-1431) in 1428 legislated that anyone who cited a Bishop in a civil court incurred an excommunication reserved for absolution to the Roman Pontiff alone, except in danger of death.[19]

However, the present application of this excommunication under the law of the Code is slightly different from the application that was provided for in the Constitution of Pope Martin V. In that Constitution the act of bringing any Bishop before a civil judge was punished with an automatic (*ipso facto*) excommunication from which the Pope alone could absolve. Today the excommunication reserved in a special manner to the Holy See is incurred only by one who cites his own Ordinary in civil court without permission. To cite a Bishop other than one's own Ordinary is punished today with an excommunication simply reserved to the Holy See.[20]

The privileged forum of the Episcopate forbids the bringing of a Bishop before a civil court as a defendant in any case whether contentious or criminal.[21] It is enjoyed by all who have been promoted to the Episcopate, even before they have received consecration.[22]

The word "*conveniri*" of canon 120, § 1, has the judicial signification of forcing a person to appear before a judge as a debtor or an

[16] Sess. XIII, *de ref.* c. 6. cf. Schroeder, *Council of Trent,* pp. 360, 361.

[17] *Fontes,* n. 1099.

[18] Const. *Apostolicae Sedis,* 12 oct. 1869, § 1, n. 7.—*Fontes,* n. 552.

[19] Const. *Ad reprimendas,* 1 febr. 1428, § 4—*Fontes,* n. 46.

[20] Canon 2341.

[21] Canon 120, §§ 1, 2.

[22] Bouix, *Tractatus de Episcopo* (2 vols., Parisiis, 1873), p. 338 (hereafter cited *De Episcopo*).

accused party.[23] Hence, the privilege does not require that the faithful obtain the permission of the Holy See in order to bring a Bishop into civil court as a witness, as a procurator or as an expert.[24] But care must be exercised in such actions in order that any and all danger of irreverence to the clerical state be absent.[25]

The danger of irreverence may be increased when the Bishop is brought before a civil tribunal as a witness in a criminal trial. For trials of this nature may often cast a shadow on the character of witnesses and others involved in them. Hence the obligation of reverence toward the Episcopate, since it is based on the divine law, may prevent the summoning of a Bishop into a civil tribunal, even in those circumstances in which the privilege of the forum does not render him immune from citation.[26]

The law asserting this privilege allows for legitimate contrary provisions in particular territories.[27] Such contrary provisions arise mainly from concordats.[28] Still custom, since it exists as a legitimate instrument of law,[29] may become a source of a contrary provision that would be capable of abrogating in a particular country the general law of the privileged forum.[30]

In the United States there exists in fact a practice derogatory to the privileged forum. Ayrinhac (1867-1930) in an article written before the publication of the Code,[31] held that this practice had abrogated the privilege of the forum in America. Hynes,[32] maintains that this practice has received the tacit consent, at least as regards the forum of priests and minor clerics, thus abrogating

---

[23] Beste, *Introductio*, p. 177.

[24] Vermeersch-Creusen, *Epitome*, I, n. 242; Cappello, *Summa*, n. 255; Wernz-Vidal, *Ius Canonicum*, II, n. 76.

[25] Canon 119.

[26] Coronata, *Institutiones*, I, n. 183; Wernz-Vidal, *Ius Canonicum*, II, n. 79.

[27] Canon 120, § 1: ". . . nisi aliter pro locis particularibus legitime provisum fuerit."

[28] Vermeersch-Creusen, *Epitome*, I, n. 242.

[29] Canons 25-30.

[30] Chelodi, *Ius de Personis*, n. 111; Blat, *Commentarium*, II, n. 56; Coronata, *Institutiones*, I, n. 183.

[31] Ayrinhac, "The Motu Proprio *'Quantavis Diligentia'*"—*ER*, XLVII (1912), 303-316.

[32] *The Privileges of Cardinals*, p. 113.

for them the privileged forum. This contention seems difficult to uphold. For the American legal procedure of ignoring the privileged forum does not seem to have received even tacit consent which would enable it to abrogate the clerical privilege of the ecclesiastical forum.

It is true that the Bishops of the United States, though they could have objected, have been silent in this matter. But the silence seems to be a silence of prudence dictated by the necessity of forestalling greater evils, such as the bringing of opprobrium on the Church by insistence on the clerical privilege of the ecclesiastical forum. Such silence can hardly be interpreted as tacit consent, but rather as mere toleration of a practice which for the present can not be opposed.[33] Under such circumstances the American practice should not be considered as adequate for the abrogation of the privileged forum in this country.

Furthermore, the very existence of the practice would not abrogate the privileged forum if the practice were unreasonable. It is difficult to see how such a practice could be reasonable. For it would not necessarily promote the general good or safeguard the freedom and dignity of the hierarchy, which it would be expected to accomplish if it were to be considered reasonable.[34] The time element does not render a practice reasonable. The Sacred Congregation of the Council[35] declared a custom of 170 years of employing laymen as co-judges in matrimonial trials as unreasonable, since laymen, according to the general law, cannot exercise ecclesiastical jurisdiction.[36]

In a similar way, the civil judge in the United States when sitting in judgment on clerics is exercising jurisdiction which belongs to church courts, and it, therefore, seems that custom cannot be invoked here, for the judge's action would be unreasonable in

---

[33] Van Hove, *Commentarium Lovaniense in Codicem Iuris Canonici,* Vol. I, tom. III, *De Consuetudine, De Temporis Supputatione* (Mechliniae-Romae: H. Dessain, 1933), n. 66 (hereafter cited *De Consuetudine*); Cappello, *Summa,* I, n. 111.

[34] Van Hove, *De Consuetudine,* n. 96; Regatillo, *Institutiones,* I, n. 113.

[35] Resolutio, Wratislavien, 14 dec. 1918—*AAS,* XI (1919), 128. Cf. Bouscaren, *Digest,* I, 97-98.

[36] Canon 118.

these cases. Lydon, who has revised a post-Code work of Ayrinhac,[37] seems to teach that the practice of the American Judiciary in ignoring the privileged forum is unreasonable, and hence has not abrogated the privileged forum in the United States.

Following Beste[38] and Wernz (1842-1918)-Vidal (1868-1939),[39] the writer holds that the privilege of the forum, though not recognized in American Civil Law, still binds the faithful of the United States, and places on them the obligation of obtaining the necessary permission before citing a cleric in civil court. This stand seems to have been confirmed by a declaration of the Sacred Congregation of the Council to the effect that a certain E. J. Daignault and his associates of Woonsocket, Rhode Island, incurred the excommunication of canon 2341, which is reserved in a special manner to the Holy See, for neglecting to obtain the necessary permission before citing in civil court their Ordinary, William Hickey, Bishop of Providence.[40]

Hynes,[41] following Downs,[42] maintains that this declaration indicates that the privilege of the forum has not been completely abrogated in America, and that the custom has not derogated the privileged forum of major American ecclesiastics such as Cardinals and Bishops, though it has derogated the privileged forum of subordinate clerics. This interpretation, if followed to its ultimate conclusion, would give rise to a rather strange condition in the United States. There would exist only the privileged forum of one's proper Ordinary, as this declaration mentions only the penalty attached to the act of citing one's proper Ordinary in civil court without the proper permission. Thus a Bishop Ordinary would enjoy the privilege of the forum when cited by his own subjects, but not

---

[37] *Penal Legislation in the New Code of Canon Law* (revised by P. J. Lydon, New York: Benziger Brothers, 1936), p. 217 (hereafter cited *Penal Legislation*).

[38] *Introductio*, p. 177.

[39] *Ius Canonicum*, II, n. 77.

[40] *AAS*, XX (1928), 146.

[41] *The Privileges of Cardinals*, p. 113.

[42] *The Concept of Clerical Immunity*, The Catholic University of America Canon Law Studies, n. 126 (Washington, D. C.: The Catholic University of America Press, 1941), p. 50 (hereafter cited *Clerical Immunity*).

when cited by persons other than his subjects. Obviously this is not the intent of the declaration.

The better interpretation seems to be that the Holy See looked upon this case as involving a prominent figure, the Bishop of a diocese, and utilize it as an opportunity for establishing the fact that a custom contrary to the privileged forum of clerics may not be tolerated in the United States. This interpretation is rendered all the more tenable, since it is difficult to see how the plaintiffs in the case could have incurred the automatic excommunication enacted in canon 2341, if legitimate custom had exempted them from this penal law.[43] Moreover, the privilege of the forum is a single concept, as can be seen through a comparison of canon 108 with canon 120. It is not composed of two separate privileges. The Episcopal ecclesiastical forum, though the observance of it is imposed under more stringent requirements and penalties, is substantially the same as that of other clerics.[44] Thus the declaration of the Sacred Congregation of the Council, when it mentioned the specific penalty incurred, was not vindicating a privileged forum only for major ecclesiastics but rather for all clerics in the United States.

The cases comprehended under this privilege are all temporal cases, whether contentious or criminal, in which Bishops are involved as defendants. The privilege extends only to temporal cases, as all spiritual cases involving either the clergy or the laity are subject to the competence of the church court not by privilege but by the nature of the case itself.[45] The cases in which Bishops are involved as plaintiffs are not subject to this privilege, as the plaintiff follows the forum of the defendant.[46] Thus a Bishop in suing a layman may, for example, bring him into a civil court. Naturally,

---

[43] Ayrinhac, *Penal Legislation,* p. 217.

[44] Coronata, *Institutiones,* I, n. 183.

[45] Canon 1553, § 1: Ecclesia iure proprio et exclusivo cognoscit: 1° De causis quae respiciunt res spirituales et spiritualibus adnexas: Cf. Solieri, *Institutiones,* pp. 168-170, Lega, *Commentarius in Iudicia Ecclesiastica iuxta Codicem Iuris Canonici* (curante V. Bartoccetti, 3 vols., Vol. I, 1938; Vol. II, 1939; Vol. III, 1941; Romae: Anonima Libraria Cattolica Italiana), I, 12 (hereafter cited *Commentarius in Iudicia*).

[46] Canon 1559, § 3: "Actor sequitur forum rei; . . ."

if the defendant enjoys the privilege of the forum, the Bishop would be bound to cite him in the church court.

ARTICLE II. SPECIAL FORUM ENJOYED BY BISHOPS AS DEFENDANTS IN CRIMINAL CASES

In view of the exclusive competence of its tribunals over all litigation in which clerics are involved as defendants, it remains for the Church to determine the limits of competence enjoyed by the individual ecclesiastical tribunals. These limits are set forth in canons 1556-1568.

Competence implies a definite jurisdiction by which certain judges or tribunals are empowered to hear specific cases. It is the circumscription of a tribunal's power by which is determined the amount or share of jurisdiction given to any one judge or court. Objectively, then, competence constitutes the potential sphere of activity of a given judge or tribunal.[47] It is variously determined according to the persons involved in the suit, the nature of the case and the territory within which the defendant has a domicile or quasi-domicile.[48]

In establishing the limits of judicial jurisdiction on the grounds of the person involved, the Church has reserved to the exclusive competence of the Roman Pontiff all criminal trials in which Bishops are defendants, and likewise the criminal trials of those who have been appointed to the Episcopacy but not yet consecrated.[49] This reservation renders all tribunals, even the tribunals of the Holy See, absolutely incompetent to hear these cases.[50]

The distinction between civil and criminal trials is similar in both canon and secular law. The civil trial deals with disputed

---

[47] Roberti, *De Processibus* (2 vols., Vol. I, 2. ed., 1941; Vol. II, 1927; Romae: *Custodiam Librariam Pontificii Instituti Utriusque Iuris*), I, n. 60 (hereafter cited *De Processibus*).

[48] Burke, *Competence in Ecclesiastical Tribunals,* The Catholic University of America Canon Law Studies, n. 14 (Washington, D. C.: The Catholic University of America, 1922), p. 6.

[49] Canon 1557, § 1, 3°; Blat, *Commentarium,* IV, n. 12.

[50] Canon 1558; Raus, *Institutiones Canonicae iuxta Novum Codicem Juris pro Scholis vel ad Usum Privatum synthetice Redactae* (2. ed., Parisiis: Typis Emmanuelis Vitte, 1931), n. 98 (hereafter cited *Institutiones*).

rights and claims, as well as damage caused by negligence (civil torts). Criminal trials have an offense against society as their proper object. In civil suits private persons, either physical or moral, implore the protection of the courts against other persons who impugn their rights and claims. In criminal suits the Church (or the State, respectively) through its officers accuses the defendant of an offense and seeks proof of that offense in order to obtain a sentence declaring or inflicting a penalty on the defendant.[51] Thus, whenever the Church accuses a Bishop of an offense, there is occasioned a criminal trial which is reserved to the competence of the Roman Pontiff.

In the early centuries of the Church Bishops enjoyed, as was noted in the historical sketch of the privileged forum,[52] a complete exemption from the jurisdiction of the civil courts. But within the Church itself Bishops enjoyed little exemption even from the competence of local tribunals. In the second century, for example, a certain Marcion, Bishop of Pontus, was excommunicated by the presbyterium, a body of priests who served as a senate to the Bishop.[53]

Toward the end of the third century Bishops were indirectly subject to many forums. Bishops who enjoyed the favor of the Emperor traveled about the country handling the cases of other Bishops, often disposing of them on no better ground than that of personal enmity.[54] St. Athanasius (295-373), Bishop of Alexandria, (328-373), received such treatment, and attempts were even made to prevent him from appealing his condemnation to the Roman Pontiff.[55] Such situations as this probably were the occasion of the legislation of the Council of Sardica (343), which vindicated for Bishops their right to appeal sentences passed on them to the

---

[51] Woywod, "Procedural Law of the Church"—*The Homiletic and Pastoral Review* (New York, 1900-), XXX (1930), 729.

[52] *Supra*, pp. 43-45.

[53] St. Ambrosius, *De Officio*—Migne, *Patrologiae Cursus Completus, Series Latina* (221 vols., Parisiis, 1844-1864), III, 139 (hereafter cited *MPL*).

[54] Schroeder, *Disciplinary Decrees*, pp. 64, 65.

[55] McSorley, *An Outline History of the Church by Centuries* (St. Louis: B. Herder Book Co., 1944), pp. 76, 95, 106 (hereafter cited *History of the Church*); St. Hilary, Fragmentum, V, no. 2, *MPL*, X, 683.

Roman Pontiff.[56] This right of appeal seems to be the early forerunner of the subsequent practice of reserving Episcopal cases to the papal forum.

In the late fourth and early fifth century, Popes and Emperors were in conflict over the right of removing or condemning Bishops.[57] These conflicts, though they were primarily concerned with freeing the Episcopate from the influence of the civil arm, indicated at least the need of handling these cases in a special manner. The manner that evolved in this period was not the reservation of Episcopal cases to the Holy See. It was trial before a council, local or provincial. The Council of Riez (439) deposed a certain Bishop Armentarius who, contrary to the ruling of the Metropolitan Hilary of Arles (+ 449), had been consecrated by two Bishops who were not metropolitans.[58] The I General Council of Constantinople (381), in deposing a certain Maximus, a claimant to the See of Constantinople,[59] indicated an acceptance of this method of handling Episcopal cases. Canons 9 and 17 of the Council of Chalcedon (451)[60] established the jurisdiction of the Metropolitan, and of the metropolitan or provincial councils, to hear cases of the Episcopate in the five major dioceses of the Eastern Empire.[61]

In the West this method received little recognition. St. Gregory of Tours (538-594) tells of Bishops who, on losing the favor of the Emperor, were prevented by him from ruling the dioceses for which they were consecrated.[62] By the ninth century this type of

---

[56] C. 4 (c. 10, C. III, q. 6)—Mansi, III, 7.

[57] Pope St. Liberius (352-366) and the Emperor Constantius (337-361) clashed over the condemnation of St. Athanasius, Bishop of Alexandria—F. Mourret, *A History of the Catholic Church* (6 vols., St. Louis: B. Herder Book Co., 1946-1947, translated by N. Thompson), II, pp. 151-155; Mansi, III, 201. Pope Innocent I (401-417) protested to no avail the exile of St. John Chrysostom (ca. 354-407), Bishop of Constantinople (398-404)—Thomassinus, *Vetus et Nova Ecclesiae Disciplina circa Beneficia et Beneficiarios* (3 toms. in 10 vols., Magontiaci, 1787), Pars I, lib. I, cap. 10, n. 10 (hereafter cited as Thomassinus).

[58] Mansi, V, 1192.

[59] C. 4—Schroeder, *Disciplinary Decrees,* p. 67.

[60] Schroeder, *Disciplinary Decrees,* pp. 98, 116.

[61] Thomassinus, Pars I, lib. I, cap. 10, n. 12.

[62] *Historia Francorum,* Lib. IV, c. 18—*MPL,* LXXI, 284; Lib. V, c. 5—*MPL,* LXXI, 321.

lay domination became one of the greater evils oppressing the Church. The pseudo-Isidorian decretals (circa 847-852) aimed at destroying this evil[63] by establishing the practice of reserving criminal cases involving Bishops to the tribunals of Rome. Through the use of spurious documents, the authors of these decretals tried to obtain for this practice the standing of an early Church procedure.[64]

This work accomplished its purpose, for its forgeries were not discovered to be such until the fifteenth century,[65] with the result that Pontiffs of the centuries following the publication of these decretals often enacted their provisions into law. Pope St. Nicholas (865) by means of a general enactment reserved the condemnation of a Bishop to Rome.[66] This reservation, first promulgated for the whole Church at that time, was repeated by later Pontiffs with minor changes.[67] Pope Boniface VIII (1294-1303) recognized this forum in declaring that the Inquisition[68] could not proceed without a special mandate against a Bishop either on the suspicion of or in

[63] Van Hove, *Prolegomena*, pp. 306-307.

[64] E.g., c. 5, C. III, q. 6 (a letter to a *Chorepiscopus*, Gratus, attributed to Pope Sixtus II [257-258]—Jaffé, n. 133); c. 1, C. XI, q. 1 (a letter to a certain Bishop Felix, attributed to Pope Caius [283-296]—Jaffé, n. 157).

[65] Van Hove, *Prolegomena*, p. 311.

[66] C. 10, C. III, q. 6 (letter to Salaman, King of the Bretons—Jaffé, n. 2789).

[67] "Hoc autem nolo vos lateat non debere praeter sententiam Romani Pontificis universale concilium celebrari aut episcopos demnari vel deponi; etsi licet vobis aliquos examinare, definitivam tamen sententiam absque consulto Romani Pontificis, ut dictum est, non licet declarare quod in sanctis canonibus statutum, si queritur, potestis invenire. . . ."—ep. *Cum ex venerabilium* (Dec. 17, 1053) of Pope St. Leo IX—*Bullarum Diplomatum et Privilegiorum Sanctorum Pontificum Taurinensis Editio* (24 vols. in 25, Augustae Taurinorum, 1857-1872), I, 626 (hereafter cited *Bull. Rom.*).

"Episcopi quoque a metropolitanis suis munus consecrationis accipiunt, qui tamen non possunt nisi per Romanum Pontificem condemnari." (c. 2, X. *de translatione episcopi*, I, 7—excerpt from a letter of Pope Innocent III, given at the Lateran to the Chapter of Angers in 1199)—Potthast, n. 575.

[68] The purpose of the Inquisition was to seek out and try those who were suspected of heresy. Its authority was derived from mandates of the Holy See, which exempted the Inquisitors from the jurisdiction of the Episcopal curia, and thereby gave them practically unlimited jurisdiction in the matter of heresy. Cf. Vacandard, *The Inquisition* (translated from the 2. French

prosecuting him for the crime of heresy.[69] This was a further emphasis of the reservation of Episcopal condemnation to Rome, as the mandate which the inquisitors needed in the respective case had to come from the Roman Pontiff.[70]

The reservation to the exclusive competence of the Roman Pontiff of the right to pass a sentence of condemnation upon a Bishop was reenacted by the Council of Trent (1545-1563) in its legislation which required that all major cases involving Bishops as offenders be heard and decided by the Roman Pontiff himself.[71] If the case could not be tried at Rome, the Council provided that Metropolitans or other Bishops chosen by the Pontiff should hear the case and submit the findings to the Pope for sentence. It allowed that minor cases (those cases in which the Bishop would not be subject to the penalties of deposition or deprivation of office) be heard by a provincial council or by persons delegated by that council.[72] This practice was followed until the promulgation of the Code, as the authors who wrote after the Council of Trent testify.[73]

---

ed. by Bertrand L. Conway, New York: Longmans, Green & Co., 1915), pp. 87 ff.

[69] C. 16, *de hereticis,* V, 2, in VI° (October 1, 1298); Potthast, n. 24730.

[70] Vancandard, *loc. cit.*

[71] "Causae Episcoporum, cum pro criminis objecti qualitate comparere debeant, coram Pontifice Max. referantur, ac per ipsum terminentur"—sess. XIII, *de ref.,* c. 8. Cf. Schroeder, *Council of Trent,* p. 361.

[72] "Causae criminales graviores contra episcopos, etiam haeresis, quod absit, quae depositione aut privatione dignae sunt, ab ipso tantum summo Romano Pontifice cognoscantur et terminentur. Quod si ejusmodi sit causa, quae necessario extra Romanam curiam sit committenda, nemini prorsus ea committatur, nisi metropolitanis aut episcopis a beatissimo Papa eligendis. Haec vero commissio et specialis sit et manu ipsius sanctissimi pontificis signata, nec unquam plus his tribuat, quam ut solam facti instructionem sumant processumque conficiant, quem statim ad Romanum Pontificem transmittant, reservata eidem Sanctissimo sententia definitiva. . . . Minores vero criminales causae episcoporum in concilio tantum provinciali cognoscantur et terminentur, vel a deputandis per concilium provinciale."—sess. XXIV, *de ref.,* c. 5. Cf. Schroeder, *Council of Trent,* p. 466.

[73] Barbosa, *Iuris ecclesiastici universi libri III* (3 vols., Lugduni, 1650), Vol. I, cap. XII, n. 42; Schmalzgrueber, *Ius Ecclesiasticum Universum* (5 vols. in 12, Romae, 1843-1845), Lib. III, tit. 2, n. 74; Reiffenstuel, *Ius Canonicum Universum* (5 vols. in 6, Romae, 1831-1834). Lib. II, tit. 31, n.

The Code has removed minor criminal cases involving offenses of the Episcopate from the competence of the provincial council, thus reserving all Episcopal cases to the exclusive competence of the Roman Pontiff.[74] This reservation is such that it renders any judge absolutely incompetent to sit in judgment on a criminal case in which the defendant is a Bishop.[75] Should it happen that any inferior judge attempt to give a sentence in such a case, the sentence would be vitiated with incurable nullity.[76]

This privilege applies to all criminal cases in which Bishops are defendants.[77] If a Bishop is a plaintiff, bringing a charge of crime through the promoter of justice as the law requires,[78] the trial is held in the forum of the defendant, as the plaintiff follows the forum of the defendant.[79]

Lega (1860-1935)-Bartoccetti[80] abstain from applying the principle that the plantiff follows the forum of the defendant when the Bishop is a plaintiff in criminal procedure. They claim that the privilege according to its terms comprehends the entire trial, not the citation alone. From this they conclude that the Roman Pontiff must hear all criminal cases in which Bishops are involved either as plaintiffs or defendants. They argue that even as a plaintiff the Bishop faces a judgment in so far as the tribunal must determine whether or not the Bishop is warranted in pressing the prosecution. Thus, since the right of judging a Bishop is reserved to the Pontiff, and since the Bishop even as a plaintiff is subject to some form of

---

38; Bouix, *De Episcopo,* I, 322 et seq.; Lega, *Praelectiones in Textum Iuris Canonici, de Iudiciis Ecclesiasticis* (2 lib. in 4 vols., Romae, 1896-1901), IV, 235 (hereafter cited *De Iudiciis Ecclesiasticis*); Wernz, *Ius Decretalium* (2. ed., 6 vols. in 10, Romae et Prati, 1906-1913), V, n. 297.

[74] Canon 1557, § 1; "Ipsius Romani Pontificis dumtaxat ius est iudicandi: 3° Legatos Sedis Apostolicae, et in criminalibus Episcopos, etiam titulares." Cf. Blat, *Commentarium,* IV, n. 12.

[75] Canon 1558.

[76] Canon 1892, 1°. Cf. Chelodi, *Ius Poenale et Ordo Procedendi in Iudiciis Criminalibus iuxta Codicem Iuris Canonici* (Tridenti: Libr. Edit. Tridentum, 1925), n. 115 (hereafter cited *Ius Poenale*).

[77] Cappello, *Summa,* III, n. 14; Vermeersch-Creusen, *Epitome,* III, n. 13.

[78] Canon 1934.

[79] Canon 1559, § 3: "Actor sequitur forum rei. . . ."

[80] *Commentarius in Iudicia,* I, 33-35.

judgment, criminal proceedings even when instituted by Bishops are reserved, so they contend, to the Roman Pontiff for judgment.

But, following Vermeersch-Creusen,[81] the writer believes that this argument cannot be accepted as convincing. For the privilege was granted out of respect to the Episcopal dignity,[82] and the appearance of a Bishop in court as a plaintiff does not ordinarily constitute an act capable of bringing indignity upon the Episcopal office. It should be maintained that the privilege reserves to the Roman Pontiff only the criminal cases in which Bishops are cited as defendants. However, this does not interfere with the Bishop's right of bringing or appealing to the authority of the Roman Pontiff any case in which he is a plaintiff, since even laymen are authorized to do so.[83]

The criminal cases thus reserved are not necessarily heard by the Roman Pontiff in person. In fact, as Roberti points out,[84] it is customary to delegate some Congregation or Commission of Cardinals to hear the criminal cases which involve Bishops as defendants.

It may be asked whether or not a Bishop has the right to appeal a sentence passed on him by such a delegated Commission or Congregation. Roberti,[85] even though he acknowledges that there are reasons for an affirmative answer, nevertheless denies this right of appeal, inasmuch as the Commission or Congregation in using delegated power functions as a supreme tribunal. On the other hand, Vermeersch-Creusen[86] maintain that there always remains the possibility of seeking from the Roman Pontiff a new hearing of the case, which hearing is not refused. The writer follows the latter opinion in this matter.

The Episcopal privilege just considered reserves to the competence of the Roman Pontiff only the criminal cases which affect

[81] *Epitome,* III, n. 13.

[82] Bouix, *De Episcopo,* I, 338; Roberti, *De Processibus,* I, n. 63.

[83] Canon 1569, § 1: "Ob primatum Romani Pontificis integrum est cuilibet fideli in toto orbe catholico causam suam sive contentiosam sive criminalem, in quovis iudicii gradu et in quovis litis statu, cognoscendam ad Sanctam Sedem deferre vel apud eandem introducere."

[84] Roberti, *De Processibus,* I, n. 63.

[85] "De Foro Competenti"—*Apollinaris,* III (1930), 136.

[86] *Epitome,* III, n. 15.

any Bishop as a defendant. Another privilege is granted to residential Bishops and those titular Bishops who enjoy a status equal to that of residential Bishops,[87] by which even civil trials in which they are involved as defendants are reserved to the tribunals of the Holy See.[88] This reservation will be considered in the second part of this work. Titular Bishops as such enjoy no special forum in civil matters, but are subject to the local ecclesiastical tribunals in the same manner as priests and other minor clerics.[89]

ARTICLE III. PRIVILEGES ENJOYED BY BISHOPS WHEN ACTING AS WITNESSES IN ECCLESIASTICAL TRIALS

The Law of Justinian is the source of the present general ecclesiastical law which requires that witnesses be examined in the place where the court sits.[90] The specific place is the city or even the hall in which the tribunal habitually assembles.[91] It is from the obligation of appearing in this specific place for the purpose of giving testimony that Bishops are exempted by a privilege of the general law. However, they are bound to notify the judge of the place in which they wish to testify.[92]

This privilege does not exempt Bishops from the obligation of testifying in ecclesiastical tribunals. It merely grants them the choice of place in which they will testify.[93] The choice, however, should be dictated by reasonable consideration, so as not to place

---

[87] I.e., permanent Apostolic Administrators and the Coadjutors of a totally incapacitated residential Bishop.

[88] Canon 1557, § 2, 1°.

[89] Vermeersch-Creusen, *Epitome*, III, n. 14; Cappello, *Summa*, III, n. 14; Roberti, *De Processibus*, I, n. 63; Coronata, *Institutiones*, III, n. 1097, *nota* 9.

[90] *Novellae* (90. 5).

[91] Noval, *Commentarium Codicis Iuris Canonicis, Lib. IV, De Processibus*, Pars I, *De Iudiciis* (Augustae Taurinorum: Marietti, 1920), p. 144 (hereafter cited *De Iudiciis*).

[92] Canon 1770, § 1—"Testes sunt examini subiiciendi in ipsa tribunalis sede. § 2—ab hac generali regula excipiuntur: 1° S.R.E. Cardinales, Episcopi et personae illustres quae suae civitatis iure eximuntur ab obligatione comparendi coram iudice testificandi causa: ii omnes eligere ipsi possunt locum ubi testificentur, de quo iudicem certiorem facere debent; . . ."

[93] Lega-Bartoccetti, *Commentarius in Iudicia*, II, 700; Blat, *Commentarium*, IV, n. 278; Coronata, *Institutiones*, III, n. 1298.

too heavy a burden on the party bearing the expenses of the trial, or to provide either party with a just cause for complaint.[94]

All Bishops, residential and titular, enjoy the privilege of thus choosing the place for giving their testimony in ecclesiastical trials. Though canon 1770, § 2, 1°, does not expressly mention titular Bishops, it is safe to conclude that they are included under the unqualified term *episcopi* as used in this canon.[94a] For it is the usual practice of the Code to use a qualified term, such as *episcopus residentialis,* or *episcopus dioecesanus,* when it intends to exclude titular Bishops.[95]

Since a qualified term is not used in canon 1770, § 2, 1°, it seems more in accord with the practice of the Code to include titular Bishops within the scope of this privilege.[96] This freedom of choosing a place for testifying is likewise enjoyed by those who have been promoted to the Episcopate, though they have not received Episcopal consecration. For this privilege can be considered as one of those privileges of which canon 349, § 1, 1°, speaks as belonging to all as soon as they have received authentic notification of their promotion to the Episcopate. Further, following the reasoning of Schmalzgrueber,[97] the writer contends that a privilege which is granted in favor of a person because of his office should be enjoyed by a person immediately destined for that office. This is such a privilege, and thus should be enjoyed by all who have received authentic notification of their promotion to the Episcopate.

This privilege gives all Bishops and those who have been promoted to the Episcopate freedom to choose the place in which they will testify, whenever they are asked to appear as witnesses in ecclesiastical trials.

---

[94] Lega-Bartoccetti, *loc. cit.*

[94a] Vermeersch-Creusen, *Epitome,* III, n. 180; Regatillo, *Institutiones,* II, n. 579. The Congregation of the Sacraments in a reply for Spain included all Bishops among those free to testify in their own homes.—7 maii 1923, n. 24—*AAS,* XV (1923), 397.

[95] Cf. canons 334, § 1; 349, § 2; 957, § 1; 965; 966; 967; 1557, § 2, 1°.

[96] Lega-Bartoccetti, *Commentarius in Iudicia,* II, 700; Roberti, *De Processibus,* II, n. 345; Blat, *Commentarium,* IV, n. 278.

[97] *Ius Ecclesiasticum Universum,* Lib. IV, tit. 39, n. 277.

ARTICLE IV. THE EPISCOPATE EXEMPTION FROM THE PENALTIES OF SUSPENSION AND INTERDICT

All baptized persons, laymen as well as clerics, are subject to the coercive power of the Church, and are liable, unless expressly exempted, to the penalties attached to the violations of ecclesiastical law.[98]

The law declares, however, that Bishops do not incur the automatic (*latae sententiae*) penalties of suspension and interdict, unless they be expressly named in the laws enacting these penalties.[99] The exemption from these penalties dates back to Pope Innocent IV (1243-1254), who granted it to Bishops in order that they might not be too readily prevented from discharging the duties of their office.[100] Lega[101] explained the non-inclusion of excommunication along with the penalties of suspension and interdict in this exemption of Pope Innocent IV on the ground that the penalty of excommunication was at that time inflicted only on crimes which were so enormous that not even the dignity of Bishops was sufficient to warrant their exemption from the incurring of the penalty of excommunication. Pope Boniface VIII (1294-1303) recognized the existence of this Episcopal exemption from the enacted penalties of suspension and interdict in a decree of March 3, 1298, in which he questioned the suspension which it was claimed that a Bishop had incurred for the misuse of his power when he acted as the authorized agent for others in an election. He men-

[98] Canon 2226, § 1; "Poenae adnexae legi aut praecepto obnoxius est qui lege aut praecepto tenetur, nisi expresse eximatur."

[99] Canon 2227, § 2. "Nisi expresse nominentur, S.R.E. Cardinales sub lege poenali non comprehenduntur, nec Episcopi sub poenis latae sententiae suspensionis et interdicti."

[100] C. 4, *de sententia excommunicationis*, V. 11, in VI°: "Quia periculosum est episcopis et eorum superioribus propter exsecutionem pontificalis officio, quod frequenter incumbit, ut in aliquo casu interdicti vel suspensionis incurrant sententiam ipso facto, nos deliberatione provida duximus statuendum, ut episcopi et alii superiores praelati nullius constitutionis occasione, sententiae sive mandati, praedictam incurrant sententiam ullatenus ipso iure, nisi in ipsis de episcopis expressa mentio habeatur."—Canon 9 of the I General Council of Lyons (1245)—Mansi, XXIII, 627.

[101] *Praelectiones in Textum Iuris Canonici, de Delictis et Poenis* (2. ed., Romae, 1910), n. 117 (hereafter cited *De Delictis et Poenis*).

tioned that the law provided that Bishops could not incur the sentence of suspension unless they were mentioned in the law itself.[101a] The authors are witnesses to the continued existence of this privilege until the Code,[102] which substantially restates the privilege as granted by Pope Innocent IV.[103]

Bishops, then, are exempted from the automatic (*latae sententiae*) penalties of suspension and interdict unless they be explicitly mentioned in the law which enacts the interdict or the suspension. But they do not enjoy, as Cardinals do, an exemption from excommunication or from penalties which the law requires to be inflicted by sentence (*ferendae sententiae*).[104]

The law specifically suspends Bishops for the following: a) giving episcopal consecration without an apostolic indult;[105] b) ordaining the subject of another Bishop without proper dimissorial letters; c) ordaining their own subjects without obtaining proper letters regarding the question of the existence of canoncial impediments to ordination; d) advancing anyone to major orders without a canonical title; and e) ordaining a religious who belongs to a house of an institute outside the territorial limits of the ordaining prelate, contrary to the prescripts of canon 966.[106] The suspensions thus incurred are vindictive penalties.

The suspension for giving episcopal consecration without an apostolic indult is general, indicating a suspension from both benefice and office. It falls upon all concerned, the consecrated and

---

[101a] C. 37, *de electione et electi potestate,* I, 6, in VI°; Potthast, n. 24634.

[102] Reiffenstuel, *Ius Canonicum Universum,* Lib. V, tit. 26, n. 19; Devoti, *Ius Canonicum Universum Publicum et Privatum* (3 vols., Romae, 1837), III, 213; Santi, *Praelectiones Iuris Canonici iuxta Ordinem Decretalium Gregorii IX* (5 vols. in 2, New York, 1886), V, 341; Lega, *De Delictis et Poenis,* n. 117.

[103] Canon 2227, § 2.

[104] Coronata, *Institutiones,* IV, n. 1713; Ayrinhac, *Penal Legislation,* p. 38; Sole, *Praelectiones in Liber V Codicis Iuris Canonici, De Delictis et Poenis* (Romae: Pustet, 1920), n. 107 (hereafter cited *De Delictis et Poenis*); Hynes, *The Privileges of Cardinals,* p. 124.

[105] Canon 2370: "Episcopus aliquem consecrans in Episcopum, Episcopi vel, loco Episcoporum, presbyteri assistentes, et qui consecrationem recipit sine apostolico mandato contra praescriptum can. 953, ipso iure suspensi sunt, donec Sedes Apostolica eos dispensaverit."

[106] Canon 2373.

consecrating Bishop, as well as the Bishops who serve as co-consecrators. It can be removed only by means of a dispensation of the Holy See, and it remains until it is thus removed.[107]

In consequence of the law enacted in canon 2373, Bishops incur a suspension of a year's duration from conferring Orders whenever they confer Orders in the manner listed above from *b* to *e*. Though this canon does not specifically mention Bishops as subject to the suspension, Bishops are comprehended within its scope. For the suspension is incurred for the violation of the requirements enacted in canons 955; 966; 974, § 1, 7°; 993, 4° and 994, in which Bishops are mentioned.[108] In canon 974, § 1, 7°, Bishops are not expressly mentioned. However, mention of them is implicitly included in this canon, since Bishops alone may confer major orders,[109] and hence they incur the suspension if they advance anyone to major orders without a canonical title.

This privilege of exemption from automatic penalties of suspension or interdict is enjoyed by all Bishops,[110] and those who have been authentically notified of their promotion to the Episcopate, though they are not consecrated.[111]

This exemption extends to all such penalties when enacted in the universal or pontifical law, but not to the penalties enacted in particular law, unless that law has received the specific approval of the Roman Pontiff. Bishops, even titular Bishops, cannot be made the subject of any penalty of particular law even though they be specifically mentioned. For the Code has reserved exclusively to the Roman Pontiff the power of declaring or inflicting a penalty upon a Bishop.[112] This reservation, in fact, frees Bishops from all penalties of the particular law, excommunication included, whether

---

[107] Coronata, *Institutiones,* IV, nn. 2151, 2152; Cappello, *Summa,* III, n. 691; Ayrinhac, *Penal Legislation,* p. 279.

[108] Coronata, *Institutiones,* IV, n. 1713, *nota* 6; Ayrinhac, *Penal Legislation,* p. 284; Berutti, *Institutiones Iuris Canonici* (6 vols., Vol. VI, Taurini-Romae: Marietti, 1938), VI, n. 29.

[109] Canon 951.

[110] Wernz-Vidal, *Ius Canonicum,* VII, n. 195.

[111] The reason for including within this privilege Bishops authentically notified but not yet consecrated is the same as the reason given in the previous article, p. 58.

[112] Canon 2227, § 1; Chelodi, *Ius Poenale,* n. 26.

the penalties be automatic (*latae sententiae*), or inflicted by means of a sentence (*ferendae sententiae*). For coercive and judicial jurisdiction over Bishops has been removed from the competence of the Ordinaries.[113]

It is clear that the exemption from penalties as enjoyed by Bishops extends to both the particular and the general law. Bishops are excused from the automatic suspensions and interdicts of the general law, unless they be specifically mentioned in the law which establishes these penalties. They are excused from all penal precepts of the particular law, even though they should be specifically mentioned in these precepts.

As a concluding note on this article, consideration must be given to canon 2371. This canon in its latter part mentions that clerics who are guilty of simony in receiving or administering the sacraments incur a suspension reserved to the Apostolic See. This would not present a problem except that the same canon in its first part mentions specifically that Bishops guilty of simony in the administration of the sacraments are suspect of heresy. This has given rise to the question, "Are Bishops included in the term '*clerici*' as it appears in the latter part of the canon." Authorities do not agree on the answer. Ayrinhac,[114] Regatillo,[115] Coronata[116] consider that this suspension does not apply to Bishops. On the other hand Augustine[117] holds that a Bishop must be bound by this suspension for justice would demand that the more important party to the simony, namely the Bishop, would at least suffer the same penalty as the less important party. Vermeersch-Creusen[118] do not expressly consider the case. Thus the divergence of opinion on the part of authorities leads to the establishment of a *dubium iuris* which practically makes the case inapplicable to Bishops. In view of these facts the writer concludes that the suspension of canon 2371 does not apply to Bishops.

---

[113] Canon 1557, § 1; 2227, § 1. Cf. Vermeersch-Creusen, *Epitome*, III, n. 417; Blat, *Commentarium*, V, n. 47; Coronata, *Institutiones*, IV, n. 1713.

[114] *Penal Legislation*, p. 280.

[115] *Institutiones*, II, n. 1122.

[116] *Institutiones*, IV, 2155.

[117] *Commentary*, VIII, p. 447.

[118] *Epitome*, III, 574.

CHAPTER IV

THE PRIVILEGE OF BLESSING AND OF APPLYING THE APOSTOLIC INDULGENCES TO CERTAIN SACRAMENTALS

The law confers on Bishops the privilege of blessing certain sacramentals according to the approved formulas, and of applying to the same all the indulgences that the Holy See is accustomed to attach to such articles.[1]

Sacramentals are objects or actions employed by the Church, in some semblance of the sacraments, in order to obtain, through the Church's intercession, effects which are chiefly spiritual.[2] The blessing properly so called is a sacramental action established by the Church for the purpose of invoking the favor of God upon a person, place or thing, or for the purpose of constituting a person, place or thing as sacred and dedicated to God.[3]

These blessings are of two types: the blessing by invocation and the constitutive blessing. The former is a temporary sacramental consisting of the blessing itself, through which a favor is sought for a person, place or thing. The latter is a permanent sacramental by which the person, place or thing which receives the blessing is removed from profane or secular use, and is dedicated to the service of God.[4] The blessings that are strictly sacramentals are those which, after the manner of the sacraments, are employed by the ministers of the Church as instruments not of conferring but of invoking some good, chiefly spiritual.[5]

All Bishops enjoy a twofold privilege as regards sacramentals. They may both bless sacramentals that are reserved to certain re-

---

[1] Canons 349, § 1, 1° and 239, § 1, 5° and 6°.

[2] Canon 1144.

[3] Wernz-Vidal, *Ius Canonicum,* Vol. IV, pars I, n. 308; Beste, *Introductio,* p. 553.

[4] Cappello, *De Sacramentis,* I, nn. 84-86; Vermeersch-Creusen, *Epitome,* II, n. 462.

[5] Wernz-Vidal, *Ius Canonicum,* Vol. IV, pars I, n. 306; Vermeersch-Creusen, *Epitome,* II, n. 463.

ligious institutes for their blessing and apply to them all the indulgences usually attached to these sacramentals by the Holy See. The sacramentals which the Bishops may so bless in virtue of this privilege are listed completely in canon 239, § 1, 5°.[6] Consequently, this privilege is applicable only to the articles listed in the canon: rosaries, other prayer beads, crosses, medals, statues and scapulars approved by the Holy See.

The indulgences which the Bishop may attach to these articles are the apostolic indulgences and all the other indulgences which the various religious institutes have been empowered to impart in blessing these articles which for their blessing have been reserved to them by privileges.[7] The apostolic indulgences are those that are usually granted by the Roman Pontiffs at the beginning of their pontificate.[8] They are issued through the Sacred Penitentiary.[9]

For blessing these articles canon 349, § 1, 1°, requires that the Bishops use the formulas approved by the Church (*ritibus tamen ab Ecclesia praescriptis*). This requirement applies to all articles that have special formulas for their blessing,[10] and all Bishops in blessing such articles must make use of these formulas.[11] However, if no special formula is prescribed for the blessing of a given article, the Bishop may bless it through the use of a single sign of the cross without employing the words, *"In nomine Patris, et Filii, et Spiritus Sancti, Amen."*[12]

---

[6] S. Poenit., *Monita,* 11 mart. 1939—*AAS,* XXXI (1939), 132; Toso, *Commentaria,* Lib. II, tom. II, p. 38.

[7] Chelodi, *Ius de Personis,* n. 195; Cappello, *Summa,* I, n. 314; De Angelis, *De Indulgentiis,* n. 41.

[8] Coronata, *De Sacramentis,* I, n. 497; Cappello, *De Sacramentis,* II, n. 679; Fanfani, *De Indulgentiis,* n. 75.

[9] For the indulgence granted by Pope Pius XII, cf. S. Poenit., 2 mart. 1939 —*AAS,* XXXI (1939), 132.

[10] These formulas are found in the *Rituale Romanum Pauli V. Pontificis Maximi iussu editum aliorumque pontificum cura recognitum atque SSmi. D.N. Pii Papae XI ad normam Codicis Iuris Canonici accommodatum* (2. ed., iuxta typicam Ratisbonae: Fr. Pustet, 1929), Appendix, *Benedictiones Propriae* (hereafter cited *Rituale Romanum*).

[11] Wernz-Vidal, *Ius Canonicum,* II, n. 599, p. 751; Vermeersch-Creusen, *Epitome,* I, n. 461.

[12] PCI, 12 mart. 1929—*AAS,* XXI (1929), 170; Maroto, "De Sacris Benedictionibus"—*Apollinaris,* II (1929), 243-245.

Besides the privilege mentioned in canon 349, § 1, 1°, the residential Bishops of the United States enjoy a further privilege through their quinquennial faculties, in virtue of which they may bless with the sign of the cross and the formula, "*Benedicat haec omnia Deus, Pater, et Filius, et Spiritus Sanctus, Amen.* "All religious articles which the faithful, at the time of the pastoral visitation, request them to bless, even though these articles require different formulas for their blessing.[13]

The privilege of blessing and applying indulgences as granted to Bishops by the Code is bestowed upon them, not in view of their office of local Ordinary, but in view of their episcopal character.[14] The privilege is purely personal, and may not be delegated to anyone. The Sacred Penitentiary has declared that bishops may not delegate this faculty either habitually,[15] or by way of act (*per modum actus*), even to the Vicar General.[16] The Bishop alone may use this faculty as conferred by the privilege, but, since the privilege is personal, he may bless and indulgence these articles wherever he may happen to be.[17]

A. *Rosaries*

There are many prayer beads improperly called rosaries. There is but one real rosary, the Rosary of the Blessed Virgin Mary, the origin of which is traditionally ascribed to St. Dominic.[18] The blessing of and the imparting of the indulgence to this rosary is reserved to the Order of Preachers.[19] In view of their privilege,

[13] Quinquennial Faculties of Ordinaries of the United States, cap. V, n. 11—cf. Beste, *Introductio*, p. 987.

[14] S.R.C., 26 nov. 1919, V, ad 2—*AAS*, XII (1920), 182; Vermeersch, "Consultationes"—*Periodica*, X (1920), 95.

[15] Resp., 18 iul. 1919—*AAS*, XI (1919), 332.

[16] Resp., 10 nov. 1926—*AAS*, XVIII (1926), 500. It should be noted that a Vicar General who is also a titular Bishop enjoys this faculty in virtue of the privilege herein considered.

[17] Canon 74. Cf. Toso, *Commentaria*, Lib. II, tom. II, p. 38; Vermeersch-Creusen, *Epitome*, I, n. 184.

[18] Fanfani, *De Indulgentiis*, n. 113; Regatillo, *Ius Sacramentarium*, I, n. 744; Cappello, *De Sacramentis*, II, n. 685; Mutch, "Apostolic Indulgences and the Rosary"—*The Homiletic and Pastoral Review*, XLIII (1942-1943), 430 ff.

[19] *Rituale Romanum*, Appendix, *Benedictiones Propriae*, n. 35.

however, Bishops may bless this rosary and, since canon 933 allows a given object to be enriched under various titles with different indulgences, Bishops may moreover apply to a single rosary of the Blessed Virgin Mary the apostolic indulgences and the following reserved indulgences:

a. the Dominican Indulgence consisting of 100 days for recitation of each Our Father and Hail Mary;
b. the Crozier Indulgence consisting of 500 days for the recitation of each Our Father and Hail Mary;
c. the Brigittine Indulgence consisting of ten specific indulgences, the most familiar being 100 days for the recitation of each Our Father, Hail Mary and Apostles' Creed;
d. the indulgence of 40 years to be gained daily by members of the Confraternity of the Holy Rosary who carry on their person a blessed rosary.[20]

At this point it is to be noted that the Holy See has provided an exception to the general law in the use of the rosary enriched with various indulgences. The general law prohibits the gaining of many indulgences by one and the same act, unless the Holy See provides otherwise.[21] In the case of the rosary, however, the Holy See has provided that the faithful may gain by a single recitation of the rosary the apostolic indulgences together with the Crozier and Dominican indulgences provided that all three indulgences have been attached to the rosary used.[22]

In attaching these indulgences to one rosary, with the exception of the apostolic indulgences for which no formula has been prescribed,[23] Bishops are bound to use the various formulas prescribed

---

[20] Fanfani, *De Indulgentiis,* nn. 115, 16, *dubium* II; Cappello, *Summa,* I, n. 388; Chelodi, *Ius de Personis,* n. 195; Regatillo, *Ius Sacramentarium,* I, nn. 744, 745. For a treatment of these indulgences the reader is referred to Mutch, "Apostolic Indulgences and the Rosary"—*The Homiletic and Pastoral Review,* XLVIII (1942-1943).

[21] Canon 933.

[22] S. Poenit., resp., 14 iun. 1922—*AAS,* XIV (1922), 394; De Angelis, *De Indulgentiis,* n. 231; Fanfani, *De Indulgentiis,* nn. 35, 116.

[23] PCI, 12 mart. 1929—*AAS,* XXI (1929), 170; Regatillo, *Ius Sacramentarium,* I, n. 727; De Angelis, *De Indulgentiis,* n. 235.

by the Church for their application. For there seems to be no reason for holding that the "prescribed formula" as required by canon 349, § 1, 1°, relates only to the blessing of the object and not also to the application of the indulgence. If it related only to the blessing of the object, then a Bishop who blessed a rosary according to one prescribed formula would automatically apply the other indulgences, such as the Brigittine and Crozier.

It is true, of course, that the quinquennial faculties,[24] as given to Bishops in the United States, permit the blessing, with a single sign of the cross and a short specific formula, of many articles which demand various formulas for their blessing. But from this grant it is clear that the Sacred Congregation of Rites, even in reference to the formula for the blessings, is making an exception to the general law. The reasonable inference according to the mind of the Congregation is that, outside of the case of the pastoral visitation, the specific formulas for the blessings must be used whenever they exist. In the case of the rosary, different formulas exist for the application of the various indulgences.[25]

Furthermore, the reserved blessings are distinguished from one another not only because of their reservation to a specific religious institute but also because of the specific indulgence imparted through them.[26] Hence Bishops are obliged to use these formulas for the application of various indulgences to one and the same rosary. Residential Bishops in the United States, however, in virtue of their quinquennial faculties,[27] at the time of the pastoral visitation may bless as many rosaries as are offered for blessing with a sign of the cross and the formula, *"Benedicat haec omnia Deus, Pater et Filius, et Spiritus Sanctus, Amen."* Since this faculty is personal, residential Bishops may make use of it wherever they may be. Other Bishops may bless rosaries everywhere, but they must use the prescribed formulas established by the Church, if they wish to apply the different indulgences to the rosaries.

---

[24] Cap. V, n. 11—cf. Beste, *Introductio*, p. 978.

[25] *Rituale Romanum*, Appendix, *Benedictiones Propriae*, nn. 35, 39.

[26] Fanfani, *De Indulgentiis*, n. 115; De Angelis, *De Indulgentiis*, n. 265.

[27] Cap. V, n. 11—cf. Beste, *Introductio*, p. 978.

B. *Other Prayer Beads*

Among the prayer beads improperly called rosaries may be listed the following, the blessing of all of which is reserved to various religious institutes in accordance with the specific formulas prescribed:

a. the Chaplet of St. Brigit, proper to the Order of the Holy Saviour;
b. the Chaplet of St. Joseph, proper to the Carmelites;
c. the Chaplet of Our Lord or the Dominican Chaplet, proper to the Camaldulese Monks (this is not the rosary properly so called, which is associated with St. Dominic);
d. the Chaplet of the Most Precious Blood, proper to the Congregation of the Most Precious Blood;
e. the Chaplet of the Society of the Most Holy Rosary, proper to that Society;
f. the Chaplet of the Seven Dolors, proper to the Servite Fathers;
g. the Chaplet of the Most Holy Trinity, proper to the Trinitarians;
h. the Chaplet of the Holy Cross or the Crozier Chaplet, proper to the Crozier Fathers.[28]

When Bishops use the specific formulas approved by the Church, they may bless these chaplets and other chaplets approved by the Holy See. In blessing them, Bishops may apply thereto all the indulgences with which the Holy See is accustomed to enrich these chaplets, whether it be the apostolic indulgences or the indulgences which for their application to the chaplets are reserved to the various religious institutes.[29]

C. *Crosses, Medals and Statues*

All crosses, medals and statues may be blessed and enriched with the apostolic indulgences, provided that they are not made of tin,

[28] *Rituale Romanum,* Appendix, *Benedictiones Propriae,* nn. 4, 9, 33, 34, 37, 39, 40; De Angelis, *De Indulgentiis,* nn. 261-274, 241-248; Fanfani, *De Indulgentiis,* nn. 114, 115.

[29] Coronata, *Institutiones,* I, n. 401; Chelodi, *Ius de Personis,* n. 195; Cappello, *Summa,* I, n. 388; De Angelis, *De Indulgentiis,* nn. 41, 235, 274.

lead, glass which is inflated or hollow, or other similar material that may easily wear out or break.[30]

Bishops by privilege may bless all these articles and enrich them with the apostolic and other indulgences which the Holy See is accustomed to attach to these articles.[31] However in blessing these articles, Bishops must use the formula prescribed for their blessing. For example, they must use the formula found in the *Roman Ritual* if they wish to bless the medal of St. Benedict, a blessing proper to the Benedictines.[32]

The solemn blessing of crosses and of statues of our Lord, of the Blessed Mother and of the Saints is reserved to the local Ordinary or his delegate.[33] Bishops may solemnly bless these crosses and statues everywhere, for the privilege as stated in canon 349, § 1, 1°, is of a personal character, and hence may be used by Bishops wherever they may happen to be.[34] Again, in the solemn blessing of these crosses and statues, Bishops must use the prescribed formulas as found in the *Roman Ritual.*[35]

D. *Scapulars*

Scapulars are composed of two pieces of cloth joined together by two cords. These scapulars, the faithful wear over their shoulders as a mark of devotion.[36] There are five principal scapulars, reserved for their blessing to various religious institutes:

a. the Scapular of the Most Blessed Trinity, reserved to the Trinitarians;
b. the Scapular of the Passion of Our Lord, reserved to the Passionists;
c. the Scapular of the Immaculate Conception, reserved to the Theatines;
d. the Scapular of the Seven Dolors of The Blessed Virgin Mary, or the Black Scapular, reserved to the Servites;

---

[30] S. Poenit., *Monita,* 11 mart. 1939, ad I—*AAS,* XXXI (1939), 132.

[31] Cappello, *loc. cit.;* Chelodi, *loc. cit.*

[32] Appendix, *Benedictiones Propriae,* n. 31.

[33] Canon 1279, § 4; *Rituale Romanum,* tit. VIII, cc. 24, 25.

[34] Canon 67; Vermeersch-Creusen, *Epitome,* I, n. 184.

[35] Tit. VIII, cc. 24, 25.

[36] Fanfani, *De Indulgentiis,* n. 117; De Angelis, *De Indulgentiis,* n. 275.

e. the Scapular of the Blessed Virgin Mary of Mount Carmel, reserved to the Carmelites.[37]

These and all other scapulars approved by the Holy See may be blessed and indulgenced by all Bishops, provided that they use the specific formula established by the Church for their blessing.[38] Residential Bishops in the United States, however, in virtue of their quinquennial faculties[39] may bless and impose, or subdelegate another priest to bless and impose, with a single formula the five Scapulars mentioned above. The formula is contained in the *Roman Ritual.*[40]

When scapulars carry with them membership in certain societies, as is the case with the Scapular of the Most Blessed Trinity, of Our Lady of Mount Carmel and of Our Lady of the Seven Dolors, the name of the party invested in the scapulars is to be inscribed in the membership book of the various societies. This enrollment as members of the various societies is necessary if the benefits of being invested in the respective scapulars are to be gained.[41] Bishops, however, may invest the faithful in these scapulars without the obligation of inscribing the names of the parties in the membership books of the various societies.[42]

It should also be noted that a religious superior may not prevent a Bishop from enrolling the faithful in a scapular if its blessing and imposing happen to be reserved to his institute.[43]

Pope Pius X (1903-1914) conceded the privilege of substituting for all the scapulars approved by the Holy See, except those proper to Third Orders, a scapular medal, bearing on one side the image of

---

[37] *Rituale Romanum,* Appendix, *Benedictiones Propriae,* nn. 3, 5, 7, 8, 10; Fanfani, *De Indulgentiis,* n. 119.

[38] Canons 349, § 1, 1°, and 239, § 1, 5°. The specific blessings are found in the *Rituale Romanum,* Appendix, *Benedictiones Propriae,* e.g., nn. 3, 7, 10.

[39] Cap. V, n. 6—cf. Beste, *Introductio,* p. 978.

[40] Appendix, *Benedictiones Propriae,* n. 14; Regatillo, *Ius Sacramentarium* I, n. 753; De Angelis, *De Indulgentiis,* n. 283.

[41] Cappello, *De Sacramentis,* II, n. 686; Vermeersch-Creusen, *Epitome,* I, nn. 845, 851; Fanfani, *De Indulgentiis,* n. 120; De Angelis, *De Indulgentiis* n. 284.

[42] Canons 349, § 1, 1° and 239, § 1, 5° ". . . sine onere inscriptionis."

[43] Toso, *Commentaria,* Lib. II, tom. II, p. 38.

Our Lord showing His Sacred Heart, and on the other an image of the Blessed Virgin.[44] Since Bishops enjoy the privilege of applying the apostolic and other indulgences to medals,[45] they may bless and indulgence this medal. However, since this medal is to receive a specific blessing for each of the scapulars it replaces,[46] it is necessary that the Bishop bless it with as many signs of the cross as there are scapulars for the replacement of which the medal serves.

Nothing else is necessary in blessing this medal, as no formula other than the sign of the cross is prescribed for its blessing.[47] For example, if a Bishop wished to have the medal serve by way of replacement for three distinct scapulars, he would bless the medal with three separate signs of the cross. This medal may be used for any of the more common scapulars, such as the Carmelite Scapular, the Scapular of the Most Blessed Trinity, etc., since these scapulars are not strictly proper to the Third Orders.[48]

E. *Stations of the Cross*

In virtue of the ruling contained in canons 349, § 1, 1° and 239, § 1, 6°, Bishops may erect the Stations of the Way of The Cross by using the formula given in the *Roman Ritual.*[49] In consequence of this privilege they may erect the Stations of the Cross in any church, in any public, semi-public or private oratory, and in any religious place that is dedicated to religious or charitable purposes, such as hospitals, orphanages, etc. They do not need the permission of the superior or rector in order to erect the Stations of the Cross in places subject to rectors and other superiors. However, they should not erect the Stations of the Cross when these superiors are unwilling to have them erected in places subject to them. But, whenever they erect the Stations of the Cross, the Bishops should sign

---

[44] S.C.S. Off. (Sect. de Indulg.), 16 dec. 1910—*AAS,* III (1911), 22; De Angelis, *De Indulgentiis,* n. 292; Fanfani, *De Indulgentiis,* n. 121.

[45] Canons 349, § 1, 1° and 239, § 1, 5°.

[46] S.C.S. Off. (Sect. de Indulg.), *decret. cit.*

[47] S.C.S. Off. (Sect. de Indulg.), *decret. cit.;* Cappello, *De Sacramentis,* II, n. 687; De Angelis, *De Indulgentiis,* n. 292; Fanfani, *De Indulgentiis,* n. 121.

[48] Fanfani, *De Indulgentiis,* n. 118; De Angelis, *De Indulgentiis,* n. 276.

[49] Appendix, *Benedictiones Propriae,* n. 1.

a written document which may be kept as proof of the proper erection of the Stations of the Cross according to the form prescribed by the Church.[50]

In erecting the Stations of the Cross, neither Bishops nor priests are any longer bound by the restriction of the Sacred Congregation of Indulgences,[51] by which those who enjoyed the faculty of erecting the Stations of the Cross were forbidden to erect them in areas in which a house of the Friars Minor was located,[52] since this requirement was abrogated in 1938 by Pope Pius XI,[53] in virtue of whose decree it is sufficient for the valid erection of the Way of the Cross that the priest who is asked to do it have the proper faculty.

Today, then, there can be no doubt that in virtue of their faculty as given to them in the Code all Bishops can erect the Way of the Cross even in localities where the Friars Minor have a house. The exercise of this faculty still requires the use of the prescribed formula,[54] as contained in the *Roman Ritual*.[55] It should be noted here that the blessing of the crosses alone is essential for the valid erection of the Stations of the Cross,[56] and that the blessing is affixed to the wooden crosses, never to the images.[57]

A decree of the Sacred Penitentiary[58] has limited the power of the Minister General and other Superiors of the Friars Minor, so that now they may only delegate priests of their own order to erect the Stations of the Cross. Priests outside of the Order must obtain the faculty of erecting the Stations of the Cross directly

---

[50] Sleutjes, *Instructio de Stationibus S.Crucis* (5. ed., recognita a Fr. Bertrando Kurtschied, ad Claras Aquas: ex Typographia Collegii S. Bonaventurae, 1927), pp. 16, 17, 18, 36 (hereafter cited *Instructio*).

[51] Cf. Resp., 14 dec. 1857—*Decr. Auth. S. C. Indulg.*, n. 382.

[52] Sleutjes, *Instructio*, p. 18; "Studies and Conferences"—*AER*, XCVII (1938), 568; Fanfani, *De Indulgentiis*, n. 107.

[53] S. Poenit., decr. *Iamdiu ac saepe*, 12 mart. 1938—*AAS*, XXX (1938), 111.

[54] Canon 349, § 1, 1°.

[55] Appendix, *Benedictiones Propriae*, n. 1.

[56] S.C. Indulg., resp. 30 ian. 1839, ad 2—*Decr. Auth. S.C. Indulg.*, n. 270; Sleutjes, *Instructio*, pp. 29, 30.

[57] S.C. Indulg., resp. 28 sept. 1838, ad 4—*Decr. Auth. S.C. Indulg.*, n. 264.

[58] Decr. 20 mart. 1933—*AAS*, XXV (1933), 170-171.

from the Sacred Penitentiary. A Bishop may not delegate a priest to erect the Stations of the Cross in virtue of the privilege granted in canon 349, § 1, 1°.[59] He needs a special faculty to delegate a priest for this ministry. This faculty may be obtained from the Sacred Penitentiary.[60]

Canons 349, § 1, 1° and 239, § 1, 6°, empower Bishops in erecting the Stations of the Cross to enrich them with all the indulgences which the Holy See is accustomed to apply to this devotion. These indulgences were originally the same as the indulgences that could be gained by those who actually visited the Stations in Jerusalem. As no record of these indulgences existed, their exact number and extent were undetermined.[61] In 1931, however, the Sacred Penitentiary removed all doubt by abolishing all previous indulgences and providing that all the faithful, who with a contrite heart perform the pious exercise of the Way of the Cross, shall be able to gain:

a. a plenary indulgence as often as they shall complete the Way of the Cross;
b. Another plenary indulgence, if they receive Holy Communion on the same day, or even within a month after having made the Stations ten times;
c. an indulgence of ten (10) years for each station, if for some reasonable cause they were unable to complete the entire Way of the Cross.[62]

These, then, are the indulgences with which Bishops may enrich the devotion of the Way of the Cross when they erect the Stations of the Cross, in accordance with the formula as given in the *Roman Ritual,* in any church, any oratory, or any religious place devoted to works of charity or religion.

---

[59] S. Poenit., resp. 18 iul. 1919—*AAS,* XI (1919), 332; S. Poenit., resp. 10 nov. 1926—*AAS,* XVIII (1926), 500.

[60] S. Poenit., decr. 20 mart. 1933—*AAS,* XXV (1933), 170-171; cf. *AER,* XCVIII (1938), 175.

[61] Sleutjes, *Instructio,* pp. 47, 48; Cappello, *De Sacramentis,* II, n. 683.

[62] *Preces et Pia Opera in Favorem Omnium Christifidelium Vel Quorumdam Coetuum Personarum Indulgentiis Ditata et Opportune Recognita* (Civitate Vaticana: Typis Polyglottis Vaticanis, 1938), n. 164 (hereafter cited *Preces et Pia Opera*); S. Poenit., decr. 12 apr. 1932—*AAS,* XXIV (1932), 248-249.

F. *Blessing and Attaching to Crucifixes the Indulgences of the Way of the Cross*

The infirm and others impeded from carrying out the exercise of the Way of the Cross may gain the indulgences of this devotion by reciting certain prayers and meditating on the Passion while holding in their hand, if possible, a crucifix specially blessed for this purpose.[63]

In virtue of canons 349, § 1, 1° and 239, § 1, 6°, Bishops may bless crucifixes so that the infirm and others mentioned above may gain the indulgences of the Way of the Cross by complying with the conditions just recited. Since no special formula exists for blessing crucifixes for this purpose, Bishops, as long as they have the intention of applying the indulgences, may bless these crucifixes with a single sign of the cross.[64] Furthermore, Bishops can apply the apostolic indulgences to these crucifixes through the same sign of the cross with which he blesses them, provided that he make the intention of applying the apostolic indulgences together with the intention of applying the indulgences of the Way of the Cross.[65]

The crucifixes which the Bishops may so bless must be made of durable material. A simple cross will not suffice. An image of Christ crucified must be affixed to the cross. It is not sufficient that the image be painted upon the cross.[66]

G. *Imparting the Episcopal Blessing to the Faithful*

Canon 349, § 1, 1° through its reference to canon 239, § 1, 12°, confers on all Bishops the faculty of blessing the faithful everywhere in the Episcopal manner (*more Episcoporum*). The *Roman Pontifical* and the *Bishops' Ceremonial* determine the occasions when,

---

[63] Cf. S. C. Indulg., *Urbis et Orbis,* 8 aug. 1859—*Decr. Auth. S.C. Indulg.,* n. 387; S. Poenit., decr. 25 mart. 1931—*AAS,* XXIII (1931), 167; decr. 9 nov. 1933—*AAS,* XXV (1933), 502-503; Sleutjes, *Instructio,* p. 56.

[64] Sleutjes, *Instructio,* p. 60; Fanfani, *De Indulgentiis,* n. 112; Cappello, *De Sacramentis,* II, n. 684; Regatillo, *Ius Sacramentarium,* I, n. 737.

[65] De Angelis, *De Indulgentiis,* n. 259 (f).

[66] S.C. Indulg., resp. 8 aug. 1859—*Decr. Auth. S.C. Indulg.,* n. 387; De Angelis, *De Indulgentiis,* n. 259 (a), (b).

and the manner in which, this Episcopal blessing is to be given.[67] The *Bishops' Ceremonial*[68] mentions two blessings as proper to Bishops, the solemn blessing given in pontifical functions and the simple blessing given with the open hand. Both of these are proper to the residential Bishop in his own territory.[69]

The canons cited seem indeed to be opposed to this regulation of the Liturgical Books, and hence in accordance with the ruling of canon 2 in the Code there seems also to be abrogated the territorial restriction on the use of these blessings, so that Bishops would be allowed to give them wherever they may be, inasmuch as that seems to be the force of the word *"ubique"* as employed in canon 239, § 1, 12°. However, for the following reasons it appears that the present legislation has not abrogated the regulation mentioned above. The solemn episcopal blessing requires the use of the miter and crozier,[70] which canon 337, § 2, identifies with the exercise of pontifical functions (*pontificalia*). Now, canon 337, § 1, requires that the Bishop have the permission, at least reasonably presumed, of the local Ordinary in order to exercise pontifical functions outside of his own diocese. This canon, then, indicates that the regulation of the *Bishops' Ceremonial,* as mentioned above, is still in force to that extent.

As for the simple Episcopal blessing, the residential Bishop may allow his coadjutor or auxiliary to impart it.[71] The Sacred Congregation of Rites has ruled[72] that, even without the permission of the Ordinary, an auxiliary Bishop who is also the Vicar General can bless the people anywhere in the diocese in the manner of the residential Bishop. This applies to both the solemn and the simple Episcopal blessing. The Sacred Congregation gives as a reason for this answer the ruling of canon 370, § 2, as compared with the rulings of canons 349, § 1, 1° and 239, § 1, 12°. From this it ap-

---

[67] Cf. *Caeremoniale Episcoporum,* Lib. I, cap. II, n. 5; cap. IV, nn. 1, 2, 3, 4; cap. XXV; Lib. II, cap. XI, n. 9; cap. XXXIX.

[68] Lib. I, cap. IV, n. 1.

[69] Catalanus, *Caeremoniale Episcoporum,* I, 84; De Herdt, *Praxis Pontificalis,* I, pp. 48, 49; Nabuco, *Pontificalis Expositio,* I, 32.

[70] *Caeremoniale Episcoporum,* Lib. II, cap. XXXIX; Schulte, *Benedicenda* (New York: Benziger Bros., 1907), pp. 28, 76.

[71] Canon 351, § 4; De Herdt, *Praxis Pontificalis,* I, 48.

[72] Resp. 26 nov. 1919, ad V, 2—*AAS,* XII (1920), 180, 182.

pears that the mind of the Sacred Congregation is that the auxiliary Bishop is empowered to act in this matter not only because of the Episcopal privilege of blessing the faithful everywhere, but also because of the fact that as Vicar General he is also a local Ordinary.[73] This likewise serves to indicate that the Episcopal blessings, not only the solemn but also the simple, may be given by a Bishop only with the permission of the Ordinary of the place in which he wishes to give such blessings.

In this matter there is another blessing which according to the form wherewith it is to be imparted is proper to a Bishop. It is the blessing given with the triple sign of the cross. This is to be distinguished from the open hand blessing used by residential Bishops in imparting blessings while riding through the episcopal city, for example. This triple sign of the cross may be used by all consecrated Bishops everywhere, when giving absolution, distributing Holy Communion and blessing the people.[74]

In this matter and according to the interpretation already given, the word *"ubique"* of canon 239, § 1, 12°, implies that with the proper permission, as noted above, Bishops can impart the Episcopal blessings not only in the churches and to assemblies of the faithful, but also in every part of the diocese of the Bishop who grants the permission. However, in Rome the canon restricts these blessings to churches, pious places and assemblies of the faithful. Thus, the Bishop who has the proper permission can impart these blessings only in churches, etc., of the City of Rome.[75]

Furthermore, Bishops may not be given permission to impart these blessings in the four Patriarchal Basilicas of Rome. The reason for this is based on the limitation of the Cardinals' faculty in this matter, which limitation would certainly also restrict the like but less extensive faculty of Bishops. The restriction is indicated in a response under date of May 29, 1934, in which the Pontifical Commission for the Interpretation of the Code stated that the

[73] Canon 198, §§ 1, 2.

[74] Moretti, *De Sacris Functionibus,* I, n. 76 (7); Regatillo, *Institutiones,* I, n. 496.

[75] Canon 239, § 1, 12°. "Benedicendi ubique populo more Episcoporum; *sed in Urbe ecclesiis tantum, piis locis et fidelium concessibus;"* . . . Italics are the writer's.

Cardinals' privilege of blessing the faithful everywhere did not extend to the Patriarchal Basilicas of the City of Rome.[76]

Marota (1875-1937) explained this response.[77] He pointed out that basilicas are not comprehended under the term *"ecclesia,"* and that these Patriarchal Basilicas under the immediate jurisdiction of the Roman Pontiff serve as his cathedral and co-cathedrals, in which the use of this privilege would not be warranted.[78]

---

[76] *AAS,* XXVI (1934), 493.

[77] "Adimadversiones ad Secundum Responsum PCI die 29 maii 1934"—*Apollinaris,* VIII (1935), 51-54.

[78] Closely connected with the exercise of pontifical functions which are involved with the Episcopal privilege of blessing the faithful everywhere is the use of the throne and baldichin. Residential Bishops may erect a throne and baldichin in all the churches of their diocese, including those of exempt religious—canon 349, § 2, 3°. In order to use the throne and baldichin, any other Bishop needs the special permission of the residential Bishop, that is, permission over and above the permission to exercise pontifical functions in the diocese—canon 337, § 3. Cf. Vermeersch-Creusen, *Epitome,* I, 453; Coronata, *Institutiones,* I, n. 349, *nota* 6; *Caeremoniale Episcoporum,* Lib. I, cap. XIII. However, the residential Bishop may not grant this permission to his own coadjutor or auxiliary Bishop—S.R.C., resp. 26 nov. 1919, ad 3—*AAS,* XII (1920), 181.

CHAPTER V

Privileges That Concern the Concession and the Gaining of Certain Indulgences

An indulgence is a remission before God of temporal punishment due to sin, the guilt of which is already forgiven or wiped out. The source of indulgences is the treasury of the Church. They are granted by ecclesiastical authority in favor of the living and the dead, but to the former they are applied by way of absolution, while to the latter they are applied as potential benefits only by way of suffrage.[1] Bishops enjoy certain privileges both in the granting and in the gaining of indulgences.

Article I. The Privilege of Granting Indulgences

The act of granting an indulgence is an act of jurisdiction,[2] and titular Bishops who are without jurisdiction may not as a rule grant an indulgence in any diocese.[3] However, on the occasion of the consecration of a church or of an altar, the Code allows the consecrating Bishop, whether residential or titular, to grant an indulgence of one year to all who visit the church or altar on the day of the consecration; and for a visit on the anniversary the Bishop may grant an indulgence of 100 days.[4]

In the eleventh century there are records of the granting of

[1] Canon 911.

[2] Coronata, *De Sacramentis,* I, n. 479.

[3] S.C.Indulg., resp. 12 ian. 1847, ad 4—*Decr. Auth. S.C. Indulg.,* n. 433.

[4] Canon 1166, § 3. "Cum consecratur ecclesia vel altare, Episcopus consecrator, licet iurisdictione in territorio careat, indulgentiam concedit unius anni ecclesiam vel altare visitantibus in ipsa consecrationis die; in die vero anniversaria quinquaginta dierum, si sit Episcopus;" . . . This canon mentions only 50 days' indulgence for Bishops. However, this has been augmented by a decree of Pope Pius XII who, on the occasion of his twenty-fifth anniversary as a Bishop, decreed that in the future Bishops may grant an indulgence of 100 days instead of 50 days. Cf. S. Poenit., decr. 20 iul. 1942—*AAS,* XXXIV (1942), 240.

indulgences by Bishops on the occasion of the consecration of churches.[5] Bishop Ponce of Arles (circa 1000), when he consecrated the Church of Mountmajor, offered to all public penitents an indulgence whereby, if they visited and kept a vigil in the church, their public penance would be mitigated to the extent that they would be able to receive Holy Communion in any church. In 1026, Bishop Anselm of Milan offered a similar indulgence on the occasion of the consecration of the Church of the Holy Sepulcher in that city.[6]

It is certain that before the IV General Council of the Lateran (1215) Bishops granted rather numerous and generous indulgences in the form of the mitigation of public penance.[7] The IV Lateran Council complained about the superfluous indulgences whereby the Bishops who granted them were weakening the penitential discipline. To correct this abuse, the Council decreed that on the occasion of the dedication of a church an indulgence of not more than one year be granted, whether the church be dedicated by one or many Bishops; on the anniversary of the dedication the remission of public penance by way of indulgence was not to exceed forty days. The Council also established that as a rule not more than a forty days' indulgence be granted by Bishops on any occasion.[8]

---

[5] These indulgences were not specifically the same as the present day indulgences. They were concerned with the mitigation of public penance, and it is not certain that the Church wished to remit from its treasury the temporal punishment due to sin as is the case today. De Angelis, *De Indulgentiis*, n. 20; Fanfani, *De Indulgentiis*, n. 15.

[6] Lepicier, *Indulgences, Their Origin, Nature and Development* (3. English ed., London: Burns, Oates & Washbourne, Ltd., 1928), pp. 289-291 (hereafter cited Lepicier, *Indulgences*).

[7] Schroeder, "The Church and the Abuse of Indulgences in the Middle Ages"—*American Catholic Quarterly Review* (Philadelphia, 1876-1924), XLV (1921), 178-205.

[8] C. 62: "Ad haec quia per indiscretas et superfluas indulgentias, quas quidam ecclesiarum praelati facere non verentur, et claves ecclesiae contemnuntur, et poenitentialis satisfactio enervatur; decernimus, ut cum dedicatur basilica, non extendatur indulgentia ultra annum, sive ab uno solo, sive a pluribus episcopis dedicetur; ac deinde in anniversario dedicationis tempore quadraginta dies de injunctis poenitentiis indulta remissio non excedat. Hunc quoque dierum numerum indulgentiarum litteras praecipimus moderari, quae pro quibuslibet causis aliquoties conceduntur; cum Romanus pontifex qui

This limit of forty days on the Bishop's right to grant an indulgence was not changed by the Council of Trent (1545-1563).[9] It remained unchanged until 1903.[10] In that year the decree of the Pontifical Jubilee increased to 50 days the measure of indulgences which Bishops were empowered to grant.[11] The Code likewise gave Bishops the faculty to grant indulgences of 50 days.[12]

In 1942, the number of days was doubled by Pope Pius XII on the occasion of his twenty-fifth anniversary as a Bishop.[13] Thus, today, when a Bishop consecrates a church or an altar, he may grant an indulgence of one year on the day of the consecration, and an indulgence of 100 days on the anniversary of the consecration.

Herein the increase granted by Pope Pius XII has been applied to the measure of the indulgence which canon 1166, § 3, empowers Bishops in general to grant on the anniversary of the consecration of a church or of an altar. The question may be asked whether this is the proper interpretation of the grant made by Pius XII. The increase was specifically granted to residential Bishops.[14] If this specification were to be followed strictly, then only a residential Bishop in his own diocese would be empowered to grant an indulgence of 100 days to be gained by means of a visit to the church or the altar on the anniversary of the consecration. All other Bishops would be limited to the granting of a 50 days' indulgence, as stated in the Code.[15] However, the writer maintains

---

plenitudinem obtinet potestantis hoc in talibus moderamen consueverit observare." Cf. Schroeder, *Disciplinary Decrees,* p. 582 (c. 14, X, *de poenitentiis et remissionibus,* V, 38).

[9] Sess. XXI, *de ref.,* c. 9; sess. XXV, *de ref.,* c. 21, *Decretum de Indulgentiis;* cf. Schroeder, *Council of Trent,* pp. 415, 518.

[10] Cf. Fagnanus, *Commentaria in Quinque Libros Decretalium* (5 vols. in 3, Venetiis, 1696), in c. 14, X, *de poenitentiis et remissionibus,* V, 38, n. 15 (hereafter cited *Commentaria*) ; Vives, *De Dignitate et Officiis Episcoporum et Praelatorum, Tractatus Canonico-Moralis* (Romae: Fr. Pustet, 1895), n. 2017 (hereafter cited *De Dignitate Episcoporum*).

[11] S.C. Indulg., *Urbis et Orbis,* 28 aug. 1903—*ASS,* XXXVI (1903-1904), 319.

[12] Canon 1166, § 3.

[13] S. Poenit., decr. 20 iul. 1942—*AAS,* XXXIV (1942), 240.

[14] Cf. *AAS,* XXXIV (1942), 240.

[15] Canon 1166, § 3.

that in this case the measure of the indulgence is increased for all Bishops to 100 days. For canon 1166, § 3, allows for an exception to the general principle that the one who grants an indulgence must have jurisdiction.[16]

The Code thus permits a Bishop who is not a residential Bishop to grant, in this one case, an indulgence equal to that which a residential Bishop can grant. Since the Code makes no distinction as to whether the indulgence is granted on this occasion by a residential or by a titular Bishop, it should be held that, when the potential measure of the indulgence is increased for residential Bishops, it is also increased in this case for all Bishops.

The Code itself seems to point to this interpretation. For it appears that in canon 1166, § 3, the Code applied to all Bishops the increased faculty of granting indulgences that had been given specifically to residential Bishops on the occasion of the Pontifical Jubilee of 1903.[17]

The works of the authors consulted on this matter were published before the date on which the increased faculty was granted by Pope Pius XII, and they merely mention the 50 days' indulgence as it is specified in canon 1166, § 3.[18] De Angelis, the one author of those consulted whose work was published after the grant,[19] appears to hold that any Bishop may now grant an indulgence of 100 days on the anniversary of the consecration of a church or of an altar. For in summing up his historical note on the Episcopal faculty of granting indulgences, he states without qualification that Bishops may grant an indulgence of 100 days. This statement lends support to the writer's position, inasmuch as the note of De Angelis is concerned with a consideration of the Episcopal faculty of granting indulgences on the occasion of a consecration of a church or an oratory.

All Bishops, then, may grant an indulgence of one year when

---

[16] Coronata, *De Sacramentis,* I, n. 479; De Angelis, *De Indulgentiis,* nn. 54, 55.

[17] Cf. *ASS,* XXXVI (1903-1904), 319.

[18] E.g., Vermeersch-Creusen, *Epitome,* II (6. ed., 1940), n. 483; Coronata, *Institutiones,* II (2. ed., 1939), n. 737; Regatillo, *Institutiones,* II (March, 1942), n. 12; Fanfani, *De Indulgentiis* (1926), n. 9.

[19] *De Indulgentiis,* n. 40.

they consecrate a church or an altar, and an indulgence of 100 days to be gained on the anniversary of the consecration of either. This privilege of granting indulgences, however, is not enjoyed by those who have been promoted to the Episcopate but have not yet received the Episcopate consecration. For one who is not consecrated may not act as a valid minister of consecrations,[20] unless through the law or by way of apostolic indult he be empowered to do so. Thus those who are without episcopal consecration may not consecrate a church or an altar, and hence cannot grant the indulgences which have been considered here.

ARTICLE II. THE PRIVILEGE OF GAINING CERTAIN INDULGENCES

The Church usually determines upon certain works which must be fulfilled for the gaining of an indulgence. The ordinary prescribed works are confession, the reception of Holy Communion, a visit to some church or oratory and the recitation of some prayers.[21]

In the matter of gaining indulgences to which are attached the condition of visiting a church or a public oratory, all Bishops and the members of their household are recipients of a privilege under the Code. They may gain, by means of a visit to their own private chapels, those indulgences for the gaining of which there is prescribed a visit to some temple or public shrine in the city or locality in which the Bishop is actually sojourning.[22]

Since this privilege is enjoyed by the members of the Bishop's household, it is necessary to determine the persons who constitute that household.[23] The canonical notion of those who constitute the members of the household does not include everyone who may be staying with the Bishop. It includes only those persons, whether lay, cleric or religious, whose services are necessary to the Bishop

[20] Canons 1147, § 1; 1155, § 1. Cf. Regatillo, *Institutiones,* II, n. 6; Wernz-Vidal, *Ius Canonicum,* Vol. IV, pars I, n. 351; Many, *De Locis Sacris,* n. 11.

[21] Cf. canons 929; 931; 933.

[22] Canon 349, § 1, 1°, with reference to canon 239, § 1, 11°, which reads: "Lucrandi in propris sacellis indulgentias, ad quas acquirendas praescripta sit visitatio templi alicuius vel publicae aediculae civitatis seu loci, in quo Cardinales actu commorentur, quo privilegio etiam eorum familiares frui possunt; . . ."

[23] In the present work the term *"familiares,"* as used in canon 239, § 1, 11°, is rendered in English with the words "members of the household."

and who at the same time live permanently in the Bishop's home or on the grounds thereof.[24]

In particular, the phrase "members of the household" includes the Bishop's secretary and servants, such as the housekeeper, the maids, the cook, the personal attendants, the chauffeur, the gardener, etc.[25] These persons may gain by a visit to the Bishop's chapel all the indulgences to which is attached the condition of a visit to a church or a shrine in the locality wherein the Bishop is actually sojourning. Since this is so, what is said in regard to Bishops in the remainder of this article will apply also to the members of the Episcopal household.

The indulgences which may be gained in the Bishop's chapel are precisely those for the gaining of which a visit to a church or a shrine is enjoined as a condition. The privilege does not exempt the Bishop from performing the other works enjoined if he wishes to gain the indulgence.[26] Furthermore, the Bishop must make the visit to his chapel with some general or at least implicit intention of honoring God in Himself or in His saints and say some prayers, especially the prescribed prayer if one is imposed by the authority granting the indulgence. In the absence of a prescribed prayer, any prayer, oral or even mental, according to the Bishop's piety and devotion, will suffice for the gaining of the indulgence.[27]

It is sometimes enjoined that a visit be made to a specific church for the gaining of an indulgence. The question then is whether or not Bishops may gain such indulgences by means of a visit to their chapels. Fanfani[28] and Cappello[29] are agreed that such indulgences may be gained by means of a visit to the Bishop's chapel.

---

[24] Michiels, *Principia Generalia de Personis in Ecclesia. Commentarius Libri II Codicis Canonici. Canones Praeliminares* (87-106) (Belgium: Brasschaat, 1932), pp. 254, 255; Vermeersch-Creusen, *Epitome,* II, n. 154; Beste, *Introductio,* p. 202.

[25] Blat, *Commentarium,* II, n. 203; Toso, *Commentaria,* Lib. II, tom. II, p. 36; Berutti, "De Iurisdictione Quae Ipso Facto Iure Delegatur ad Audiendas Fidelium Confessiones"—*Ius Pontificium* (Romae, 1921-1949), XVI (1934), 57 (hereafter cited as "De Iurisdictione").

[26] De Angelis, *De Indulgentiis,* nn. 36, 41.

[27] S. Poenit., decr. 20 sept. 1933—*AAS,* XXV (1933), 446.

[28] *De Indulgentiis,* n. 41.

[29] *De Sacramentis,* II, n. 667.

Other authors are not clear on this point.[30] In their consideration of the privilege granted to religious and others, whereby these may gain such indulgences in the chapel of their institute,[31] the latter authors make the point that according to this grant an indulgence to which is attached the condition of a visit to a determined church may not be gained by these persons in their chapel. Then they mention that Bishops and Cardinals enjoy a similar privilege. From this one would be led to believe that, according to the view of these authors, Bishops and Cardinals cannot gain in their own chapel an indulgence to which is attached the condition of a visit to a determined church.

However, the fact that they use the word "similar" in describing this privilege of Bishops and Cardinals leaves the way open for interpreting their meaning in such fashion that the privileges are similar only in what may be accomplished through them, namely the gaining of local indulgences in their chapels, and that the privileges are not alike in the element of their restrictions, so that Bishops and Cardinals would be able to gain in their own chapels the indulgences to which is attached the condition of a visit to a determined church.

The writer follows the interpretation of Cappello and Fanfani. For the words "not determined" of canon 929, upon which the restriction of the privilege of religious in this matter depends, do not appear in canon 239, § 1, 11°, which grants to Bishops the privilege of gaining indulgences in their own chapels. To apply these words of canon 929 to the Episcopal privilege would be to restrict the applicable use of that privilege. But a privilege according to canon 67 may not be thus restricted. Hence it should be maintained that Bishops may gain in their chapels even those indulgences for the gaining of which a visit to a specific church is required. Thus Bishops may gain the *Portiuncula* indulgence in their own chapels.[32]

---

[30] Regatillo, *Ius Sacramentarium,* I, n. 699; Blat, *Commentarium,* II, n. 211; Wernz-Vidal, *Ius Canonicum,* Vol. IV, pars I, n. 160; Vermeersch-Creusen, *Epitome,* II, n. 218; Chelodi, *Ius de Personis,* n. 195.

[31] Canon 929.

[32] The *Portiuncula* Indulgence is an example of an indulgence which requires a visit to a specific church, namely a Franciscan church or any other

However, Bishops may not gain the Jubilee Indulgence by means of a visit to their chapels. For the Jubilee Indulgences are governed not by the general law but by their own proper law.[33] This law makes an exception in favor of Cardinals, who therefore may gain these indulgences in their own chapels. But it makes no such an exception for Bishops.[34]

The chapel in which these indulgences may be gained is any chapel which the Bishop happens to be using in the place where he is actually staying, whether for a short period of time or permanently.[35] However, the words "any chapel" must be understood and interpreted in accordance with the words *"propriis sacellis"* of canon 239, § 1, 11°. This would limit the words "any chapel" to the private oratories which Bishops are allowed to erect in all houses which they retain for the purpose of residence, whether in or outside of their diocese.[35a] Such a limitation would not seem to prevent a Bishop from erecting a chapel in a building which he intended to use for a residence of but short duration. Since he can erect a chapel in such a place, there seems to be no reason that would prevent the Bishop from gaining the indulgences that are offered in the locality of that chapel.

It is clear, then, that since indulgences vary from one locality to another, it is the city or the locality in which the Bishop happens to have a chapel that will determine the number of indulgences he may gain by a visit to his chapel.

The following schema, taken from Hynes,[36] will indicate the various indulgences which a Bishop and members of his household may gain as a result of the privilege under discussion.

---

church enjoying the *Portiuncula* privilege. De Angelis, *De Indulgentiis,* nn. 354-361.

[33] Wernz-Vidal, *Ius Canonicum,* Vol. IV, pars I, n. 165.

[34] De Angelis, *De Indulgentiis,* n. 184.

[35] Blat, *Commentarium,* II, n. 211; Maroto, *Institutiones Iuris Canonici ad Normam Novi Codicis* (2 vols., Vol. I, 3. ed., 1921; Vol. II, 1919, Romae: Apud Commentarium pro Religiosis), II, n. 861 (hereafter cited *Institutiones*); Toso, *Commentaria,* Lib. II, tom. II, p. 40.

[35a] Gasparri, *De Eucharistia,* I, n. 288; Many, *De Locis Sacris,* n. 100; Chelodi, *Ius de Personis,* n. 195.

[36] *The Privileges of Cardinals,* pp. 108, 109.

A. *In the chapel of a Bishop's permanent residence:*
   (a) All local indulgences that require a visit to any church or public oratory anywhere in the world.
   (b) All local indulgences that require a visit to any church or public oratory of that city or town.
   (c) All local indulgences that require a visit to a determined church, oratory or shrine in that city or town.

B. *In a chapel being used by a Bishop when away from his permanent residence:*
   (a) All local indulgences that require a visit to any church or public oratory anywhere in the world.
   (b) All local indulgences that require a visit to any church or public oratory of that city or town in which the Bishop is actually sojourning at the moment.
   (c) All local indulgences that require a visit to a determined church, oratory or shrine of that city in which the Bishop is actually sojourning at the moment.[37]

---

[37] This list applies to all indulgences with the exception of the Jubilee Indulgences, which, as shown above, may not be gained by a Bishop when he visits his own chapel.

CHAPTER VI

Miscellaneous Privileges

ARTICLE I. THE PRIVILEGE OF CHOOSING ANY PRIEST AS A CONFESSOR

The Code grants to all Bishops the privilege of choosing any priest as a confessor for themselves and the members of their household.[1] The basis of this privilege is found in a decree of Pope Gregory IX (1227-1241) promulgated between the years 1227 and 1234.[2] This decree allowed the Bishop to choose as a confessor any priest, whether or not he had the approval of his superior. Later the enactment of the Council of Trent (1545-1563), which required that a priest for hearing confessions have the approval of the Bishop (local Ordinary),[3] was applied to the use of this privilege. Bishops from that point forward had to choose as a confessor a priest who was approved by the Bishop for hearing confessions.[4] However, if the Bishop chose one of his own subjects as his confessor, the needed approval was contained in the Bishop's choice.[5]

The requirement of selecting a priest approved for hearing confessions was not the same as the requirement that the Bishop select

[1] Canon 349, § 1, 1°, with reference to canon 239, § 1, 2°—"Sibi suisque familiaribus eligendi sacerdotem confessionibus excipiendis, qui, si iurisdictione careat, eam ipso iure obtinet, etiam quod spectat ad peccata et censuras, reservatas quoque, illis tantum censuris exceptis de quibus in n. 1; . . ." Canon 349, § 1, 1° adds to this the clause, "etiam quod spectat ad casus Ordinario loci reservatos."

[2] C. 16, X, *de poenitentiis et remissionibus*, V, 38: "Ne pro dilatione poenitentiae periculum immineat animarum, permittimus episcopis et aliis superioribus, nec non minoribus praelatis exemptis, ut etiam praeter sui superioris licentiam providum et discretum sibi possint eligere confessorem."—Potthast, n. 9685.

[3] Sess. XXIII, *de ref.*, c. 15; cf. Schroeder, *Council of Trent*, p. 444.

[4] Cf. Fagnanus, *Commentaria*, in c. 16, X, *de poenitentiis et remissionibus*, V. 38, nn. 5-13; Barbosa, *Iuris ecclesiastici universi libri III*, Vol. I, cap. XII, n. 28.

[5] Fagnanus, *ibid.*, n. 14.

as a confessor a priest who had jurisdiction for hearing confession. For, in the period following the Council of Trent, it was necessary for validity that the confessor have the approval of the local Ordinary in addition to jurisdiction.[6] The approval was wholly territorial, limited in its effect to the diocese of the Bishop who granted it.[7] The jurisdiction could extend throughout the entire Church. Regulars, for example, enjoyed such jurisdiction.[8] But, no matter what was the extent of the jurisdiction, it was necessary that the confessor obtain the approval of the local Ordinary in order to exercise his jurisdiction in a given diocese.[9] Thus the requirement of approval, which in that period bound Bishops in the selection of a confessor, did not technically connote an absence of jurisdiction on the part of the confessor selected. For, once he was selected the confessor had jurisdiction. Nevertheless he needed the approval of the local Ordinary to act validly as a confessor.[10]

The Code abrogated the requirement of approval as found in the previous law when it legislated that Orders and jurisdiction are all that are required for the minister's act of conferring or granting a valid absolution.[11] Today a Bishop may select any priest as his confessor. If the priest chosen is without jurisdiction, he obtains it directly from the law on being selected by the Bishop.[12]

In virtue of this privilege a Bishop may select as a confessor

---

[6] Ferraris, *Prompta Bibliotheca Canonica, Iuridica, Moralis, Theologica, necnon Ascetica, Polemica, Rubricistica, Historica* (9 vols., Romae, 1885-1899), s.v. "approbatio," nn. 1-3 (hereafter cited *Prompta Bibliotheca*); Benedictus XIV, litt. encycl. *Apostolicum ministerium,* 30 maii 1753, § 8—*Fontes,* n. 425; Wernz, *Ius Decretalium,* IV, n. 757, p. 906.

[7] Cf. Gregorius XV, const. *Inscrutabili,* 5 febr. 1622, § 1—*Fontes,* n. 199; Urbanus VIII, const. *Cum sicut accepimus,* 12 sept. 1628—*Fontes,* n. 208; Clemens X, const. *Superna,* 21 iun. 1670, § 4—*Fontes,* n. 246.

[8] Cf. Barbosa, *Pastorialis Sollicitudinis sive de Officio et Potestate Episcopi Tripartita Descriptio* (Lugduni, 1656), pars II, alleg. 25, n. 24.

[9] Fagnanus, *Commentaria,* in c. 12, X *de poenitentiis et remissionibus,* V, 38, n. 79; Schmalzgrueber, *Ius Ecclesiasticum Universum,* Lib. VI, tit. 29, n. 13.

[10] Ferraris, *Prompta Bibliotheca,* s.v. "approbatio," nn. 4, 5.

[11] Canon 872.

[12] Canons 349, § 1, 1° and 239, § 1, 2°.

any priest, whether secular or religious.[13] The selection may be permanent or temporary, or made for each individual confession.[14] In fact, the Bishop's act of confessing to a priest would be equivalent to choosing him as a confessor, and that priest would thereby enjoy for that confession, at least, all the faculties conferred on the Bishop's confessor through this privilege.[15] This privilege of selection is not limited either as to the subject chosen or the place in which the choice is made. The Bishop may choose any priest, anywhere, and that priest may function as his confessor anywhere in the world.[16]

The confessor thus selected receives jurisdiction from the law to absolve the Bishop from all sins and all censures except those which are reserved in a most special manner to the Holy See,[17] and the censures which follow from a violation of a secret of the Holy Office.[18] The jurisdiction conferred through this privilege entitles the confessor, however, to absolve from the only sin reserved

---

[13] Berutti, "De Juridictione"—*Jus Pontificium,* XIV (1934), 57; Vermeersch-Creusen, *Epitome,* I, n. 461; Wernz-Vidal, *Ius Canonicum,* II, n. 599, p. 751.

[14] Blat, *Commentarium,* II, n. 203; Berutti, *loc. cit.*

[15] Berutti, *loc. cit.*

[16] Regatillo, *Ius Sacramentarium,* I, n. 411; Wernz-Vidal, *Ius Canonicum,* II, n. 599, p. 751; Vermeersch-Creusen, *Epitome,* II, n. 151; Toso, *Commentaria,* Lib. II, tom. II, p. 180.

[17] The censures reserved in a most special manner are incurred by those who destroy consecrated hosts or retain them for evil purposes—canon 2330; by those who lay violent hands on the person of the Roman Pontiff—canon 2343, § 1, 1°; by those confessors who absolve or pretend to absolve an accomplice in *peccato turpi*—canon 2367, § 1; by those confessors who violate the seal of confession—canon 2369, § 1.

[18] The obligation of observing the secret of the Holy Office binds not only the officials of the Sacred Congregation of the Holy Office, but also those engaged in the work of the Sacred Consistorial Congregation and those who take part in the process of Beatification or Canonization before the Sacred Congregation of Rites. To divulge the proceedings of these Congregations is to incur an excommunication, the absolution of which is reserved personally to the Roman Pontiff. Coronata, *Institutiones,* I, n. 332; Cappello, *De Curia Romana iuxta Reformationem a Pio X, Vol. I, De Curia Romana "Sede Plena"* (Romae: Fr. Pustet, 1911), I, 68 (hereafter cited *De Curia Romana*); Toso, *Commentaria,* Lib. II, tom. II, pp. 35, 36.

by the Code to the Holy See,[19] and from sins and censures reserved in any way to the Ordinary of the place of the confession.[20]

The faculties conferred by law on the confessor selected by the Bishop may be exercised not only in favor of the Bishop but also in favor of the members of the Bishop's household.[21] However, not every priest to whom the members of the household confess may exercise these faculties, but only the priest chosen by the Bishop. For the privilege of selecting a confessor rests not with the members of the household, but with the Bishop. It is important that he should make it clear that he consents to have a certain priest act as confessor for his household, if the latter is to be endowed with the privileged faculties.[22] The confessor of the household need not be the same as the one selected by the Bishop as his own confessor, since the Bishop is not limited as to the number of priests he may select to fulfill this office.[23]

Canon 349, § 1, 1°, in conferring this privilege, states that Bishops enjoy the same privilege as Cardinals in the selection of a confessor for themselves and the members of their household. But it adds a clause which does not appear in canon 239, § 1, 2°, to the effect that the priest selected enjoys jurisdiction even in cases reserved to the Ordinary of the place (*etiam quod spectat ad casus Ordinario loci reservatos*). At first glance, the addition of this

---

[19] Canon 894. "Unicum peccatum ratione sui reservatum Sanctae Sedi est falsa delatio, qua sacerdos innocens accusatur de crimine sollicitationis apud iudices ecclesiasticos." Sipos, *Enchiridion Iuris Canonici* (2. ed., Pécs, Hungary: Haladás, R.T., 1931), p. 249 (hereafter cited *Enchiridion*); Coronata, *Institutiones,* I, n. 235, *nota* 6; Blat, *Commentarium,* II, n. 203. This sin may not be absolved until the penitent has retracted the denunciation and has repaired, as far as possible, any damages that may have resulted therefrom. A grave and proportionate penance should be imposed—canon 2363.

[20] Wernz-Vidal, *Ius Canonicum,* II, n. 599, p. 750; Badii, *Institutiones,* I, n. 235; Vermeersch-Creusen, *Epitome,* I, n. 461; Toso, *Commentaria,* Lib. II, tom. II, p. 80; Cappello, *De Sacramentis,* II, nn. 292, 400.

[21] For the determination of the persons constituting the Bishop's household, cf. *supra,* p. ?.

[22] Cappello, *De Sacramentis,* II, n. 292; Berutti, "De Jurisdictione"—*Jus Pontificium,* XIV (1934), 58; Kelly, *The Jurisdiction of the Confessor according to the Code of Canon Law* (New York: Benziger Brothers, 1928). p. 149 (hereafter cited *Jurisdiction of the Confessor*).

[23] Blat, *Commentarium,* II, n. 203; Berutti, *ibid.,* p. 57.

clause would seem to imply that the confessor chosen by a Cardinal would not be able to absolve from a sin reserved to the Ordinary of the place, while the confessor chosen by a Bishop would enjoy such a faculty. This would make the Bishop's privilege more extensive than the Cardinal's. This certainly is not the intention of this clause, for Cardinals are to be expected to receive the most extensive privilege, since they are next in dignity to the Sovereign Pontiff himself[24] as members of the senate and as the principal councillors of the Pope.

Many of the authors consulted restate the clause as it appears in the canon and offer no commentary.[25] Blat[26] offers an explanation to the effect that the confessor selected by a Cardinal receives his jurisdiction from the law and is not subject to the limitations imposed by the local Ordinary through canon 893, §§ 1, 2. Thus there would be no need of the clause in question in the Cardinal's privilege. On the other hand, a confessor when chosen by a residential Bishop receives his jurisdiction from that residential Bishop, and the clause is necessary to extend the jurisdiction in so far as the privilege concerns places and reservations beyond his delegated authority.

This explanation does not seem to be to the point. It seems to rest on a theory that the Bishop's confessor receives his jurisdiction from the Bishop. Yet the canons granting this privilege[27] seem clear in stating that the jurisdiction comes from the law, through the phrase, "if he lacks jurisdiction," could furnish a basis for the opinion that the confessor may receive his jurisdiction from a source other than the law. However, the common opinion is that the Bishop's confessor derives his jurisdiction for hearing the confessions of the Bishop and the members of his household from the law itself when he is selected by the Bishop for this office.[28]

---

[24] Canon 230.

[25] Cappello, *Summa,* I, n. 388; Vermeersch-Creusen, *Epitome,* I, n. 461; Coronata, *Institutiones,* I, n. 401; Regatillo, *Institutiones,* I, n. 496; Wernz-Vidal, *Ius Canonicum,* II, n. 599, p. 750.

[26] *Commentarium,* II, n. 203.

[27] Canons 349, § 1, 1° and 239, § 1, 2°.

[28] Wernz-Vidal, *Ius Canonicum,* Vol. IV, pars I, n. 124; Chelodi, *Ius de Personis,* n. 195; Vermeersch-Creusen, *Epitome,* II, nn. 151, 154; Berutti,

In the light of this common opinion there seems to be no need for the inclusion of the clause, "even cases reserved to the Ordinary of the place." For such cases are clearly included within the scope of the privilege, as stated in canon 239, § 1, 2°. Kelly[29] thinks that this clause may have been added for the sake of emphasizing the possessed jurisdiction which the confessor enjoys over cases reserved to the local Ordinary, when he absolves the members of the Bishop's household. But the same reason would hold good for the Cardinals' as well as for the Bishops' privilege, since the members of either of the households are subject to the reservations of the local Ordinary.[30] Yet to acknowledge to the confessor this privileged authority, it was not deemed necessary to insert mention of it expressly in connection with the Cardinals' privilege. Thus the reason assigned by Kelly does not well explain why the clause appears only in the statement of the privilege as enjoyed by Bishops.

It seems to the writer that the clause, "even in cases reserved to the ordinary of the place," was added to the statement which delineates the Episcopal privilege with a view to emphasizing the fact that Bishops can make use of this privilege in the territory of a fellow Bishop, even though both are of equal rank in the hierarchy. A similar emphasis does not seem to be necessary in the case of Cardinals, since they are of the highest rank next to the Sovereign Pontiff and above local jurisdiction.[31]

ARTICLE II. THE PRIVILEGE OF PREACHING THE WORD OF GOD EVERYWHERE

The office of preaching the Word of God is proper to the Bishop in his own diocese.[32] No one may exercise this office except through a special commission from his superior, or through appointment

"De Jurisdictione"—*Jus Pontificium,* XIV (1934), 57; Cappello, *De Sacramentis,* II, n. 292; Regatillo, *Ius Sacramentarium,* I, n. 411.

[29] *Jurisdiction of the Confessor,* p. 150.

[30] Berutti, *loc. cit.*

[31] Cf. canons 230; 1557, § 1, 2°; 2227, §§ 1, 2. The latter two canons remove Cardinals from the jurisdiction of local tribunals and free them from the penalties inflicted by local Ordinaries as well as from all penalties of the general law in which they are not mentioned.

[32] Canon 1327, § 1.

by the latter to a post to which is attached the duty of preaching. Bishops enjoy a privilege in this regard, whereby they may preach the Word of God everywhere with at least the presumed consent of the local Ordinary.[33] The privilege thus granted consists in the authorization to preach on the presumed consent of the local Ordinary. The regulation of the general law requires that anyone who wishes to preach in a diocese must obtain the consent (not presumed) of the local Ordinary.[33a]

To determine the extent of this privilege it is necessary to determine the meaning of the words "presumed consent." Most of the commentators consulted[34] state without commentary that the Bishop may preach everywhere with the presumed consent of the local Ordinary. Blat[35] defines presumed consent as that consent which, at least, would not be denied if it were sought. Cappello[36] claims that the presumed consent in this case would hardly ever be lacking.

Using the definition of Blat and the statement of Cappello as a norm, the writer maintains that this privilege entitles a Bishop to preach anywhere, except in that place in which he is certain that the local Ordinary would refuse him permission to preach.

ARTICLE III. THE PRIVILEGE OF EXEMPTION FROM THE ECCLESIASTICAL PROHIBITION OF BOOKS

The ecclesiastical prohibition of books forbids the publication, the reading, the retention, the selling and the translation of books dangerous to faith or morals, as well as the communication of such books to others by any means whatsoever.[37]

Historically Bishops and other prelates have been exempted from

---

[33] Canons 349, § 1, 1° and 239, § 1, 3°. "Verbum Dei ubique praedicandi; . . ." Canon 349, § 1, 1°, has added to this privilege the limitation, "cum consensu saltem praesumpto Ordinarii loci."

[33a] Canons 1337; 1338, §§ 2, 3.

[34] E.g., De Meester, *Compendium,* II, n. 307; Wernz-Vidal, *Ius Canonicum,* II, n. 599, p. 751; Vermeersch-Creusen, *Epitome,* I, n. 461.

[35] *Commentarium,* II, n. 374.

[36] *Summa,* I, n. 388.

[37] Canon 1398, § 1. "Prohibitio librorum id efficit ut liber sine debita licentia nec edi, nec legi, nec reteneri, nec vendi, nec in aliam linguam verti, nec ullo modo cum aliis communicari possit."

this prohibition.[38] However, in certain periods of the life of the Church, Bishops have been bound by this prohibition. Especially was this the case in the times of heresy. The II Council of Nicaea (787) ordered that Bishops be deposed if they were found concealing Iconoclast literature.[39]

The next legislation in this matter as it concerned Bishops appeared with the advent of Protestantism in the 16th century. Pope Leo X (1513-1521) proscribed the works of Luther for all the faithful, even the Bishops.[40] Later, The Council of Trent (1545-1563) recommended that the Pope give a specific decree on the prohibition of books.[41] Pope Pius IV (1559-1565), in accord with this recommendation, published an Index on the prohibition of books and from the rules attached thereto no exemptions were granted. All ecclesiastics, no matter what their grade, order or dignity, were forbidden to read the books on this *Index*.[42] This same prohibition was repeated by later Pontiffs.[43]

The Code has removed this prohibition as regards the Episcopate. All Bishops, residential as well as titular, from the moment they receive authentic notification of their promotion to the Episcopate may read and retain forbidden books provided that they observe the necessary precautions.[44]

The use of this privilege is limited by the necessary precautions which canon 1401 mentions but does not determine. But since canons 1405, § 1, and 1403, § 2, must always be observed,[45] Bishops

---

[38] Pernicone, *The Ecclesiastical Prohibition of Books,* The Catholic University of America Canon Law Studies, n. 72 (Washington, D. C.: The Catholic University of America, 1932), p. 196.

[39] C. 9—Mansi, XIII, 429; Schroeder, *Disciplinary Decrees,* p. 527.

[40] Const. *Exsurge Domine,* 15 iun. 1520, § 2—*Fontes,* n. 75.

[41] Sess. XXV, *de ref.,* c. 21, *De Indice Librorum et Catechismo, Breviario et Missali;* cf. Schroeder, *Council of Trent,* p. 519.

[42] Const. *Dominici gregis,* 24 mar. 1564, § 3—*Fontes,* n. 105.

[43] E.g., Piux IX (1846-1878), const. *Apostolicae Sedis,* 12 oct. 1869, § 1, nn. 1-2—*Fontes,* n. 552.

[44] Canon 1401. "S.R.E. Cardinales, Episcopi, etiam titulares, aliique Ordinarii, necessariis adhibitis cautelis, ecclesiastica librorum prohibitione non adstringuntur."

[45] Vermeersch-Creusen, *Epitome,* II, nn. 735, 736; Cappello, *Summa,* II, n. 511.

may read forbidden books provided that: (1) these books are not for them an imminent occasion of spiritual harm, and (2) that they see to it that such books do not fall into the hands of those not permitted to read them.[46] In other words, the privilege implies that a Bishop may read forbidden books as long as, according to the dictates of the natural law, he has removed any cause of spiritual danger either to himself or to others.[47]

In bringing to a close the consideration of the privilege common to all Bishops, it is worthy of note that the Sacred Congregation of Ceremonies on December 13, 1930, extended to all Bishops, residential and titular, the title of "Your Most Reverend Excellency."[48]

---

[46] A residential Bishop may give his subjects, in urgent circumstances, permission to read certain books that are forbidden. Canon 1406, § 1.

[47] Blat, *Commentarium,* III, n. 290.

[48] *AAS,* XXIII (1931), 22.

PART II

Privileges Common to Residential Bishops

CHAPTER VII

Special Forum Enjoyed by Residential Bishops as Defendants in Contentious Trials

ARTICLE I. GENERAL INTRODUCTION TO PART TWO

The privileges considered in this part of the dissertation are those which are attached to the office of Episcopal Ordinaries. Though they are personally enjoyed by all the incumbents of this office, they are, nevertheless, real privileges. For it is the property of a real privilege to be conceded for use to the person who exercises dominion over the office, dignity, or thing to which the privilege adheres.[1]

The Code lists as Ordinaries both residential Bishops and Administrators,[2] a term which comprehends titular Bishops serving as Apostolic Administrators.[3] As a general occurrence, titular Bishops are not Ordinaries. However, since the term "Ordinary" is reserved in law for those who have ordinary power in both the internal and the external forum,[4] titular Bishops who serve as Coadjutors to totally disabled Bishops may be considered as Ordinaries, even though their office as such is not mentioned in canon 198, § 1. For by canon 351, § 2, they have all the rights and duties of the residential Bishop, and this certainly confers upon them jurisdiction in both the internal and the external forum.[5] Since, then, residential Bishops, Apostolic Administrators and

[1] Van Hove, *De Privilegiis*, n. 264; Vermeersch-Creusen, *Epitome*, I, n. 179, 5°.

[2] Canon 198, § 1.

[3] From canon 315, § 1, it is clear that permanent Apostolic Administrator enjoys the status of a residential Bishop. From canon 315, § 2, 1°, it is clear that the temporary Apostolic Administrator has the status of a *vicar capitular* who is an Ordinary. Cf. McDonough, *Apostolic Administrators*, pp. 112, 162, 163.

[4] Wernz-Vidal, *Ius Canonicum*, II, n. 367; Cappello, *Summa*, I, 263; Beste, *Introductio*, p. 216.

[5] Cf. Lynch, *Coadjutors*, p. 76.

Coadjutors of a totally disabled Bishop are Ordinaries, they enjoy most of the privileges considered in this part of the work.

The use of these privileges does not depend upon Episcopal consecration. For they are real privileges which may be used from the moment the incumbent takes possession of his office.[6] Hence, as soon as the appointee presents his Apostolic Letter of appointment to the diocesan consultors,[7] he takes canonical possession of his office and may use the privileges attached thereto, even though not consecrated.[8] In like manner Apostolic Administrators and Coadjutors of a totally disabled Bishop may make use of these privileges from the moment they present their letters of appointment to the Bishop or the diocesan consultors, since this is the method by which such Bishops take possession of their office.[9] The privileges concerned are the following:

a) reservation of the contentious cases in which residential Bishops are defendants to the competence of the Sacred Roman Rota;
b) the granting of 100 days' indulgence;
c) the granting of the Papal Blessing with an attached plenary indulgence;
d) the establishing of daily and perpetually privileged altars;
e) the precedence of residential Bishops within their own dioceses;
f) the naming of the residential Bishop in the Canon of the Mass;
g) burial within the confines of the cathedral church.

ARTICLE II. SPECIAL FORUM ENJOYED BY RESIDENTIAL BISHOPS IN CONTENTIOUS TRIALS

Residential Bishops enjoy a special forum when involved in contentious litigation. The common method for determining the competent judge in contentious matters is found in canons 1560 to 1570.[10] Canon 1557, § 2, 1°, reserves the contentious trials of resi-

---

[6] Van Hove, *De Privilegiis*, n. 264; Regatillo, *Institutiones*, I, n. 166.

[7] Canon 334, § 3.

[8] Canon 349, § 2. Coronata, *De Sacramentis*, I, n. 479.

[9] Canons 313, §§ 1, 2 and 353, §§ 2, 3.

[10] Lega-Bartoccetti, *Commentarius in Iudicia*, I, 36.

dential Bishops to the tribunals of the Holy See, specifically to the Sacred Roman Rota.[11]

The contentious cases so reserved are those in which residential Bishops are cited as defendants. Lega-Bartoccetti,[12] arguing from an analogy with canon 1572, § 2, in which no distinction is made as to whether the Bishop be plaintiff or defendant, claim that all contentious cases in which residential Bishops are involved either as plaintiff or defendant are reserved to the Rota. But this stand is contrary to the common opinion which holds that the principle, "the plaintiff follows the forum of the defendant,"[13] applies in contentious cases in which the Bishop is the plaintiff.[14] The common opinion will be followed in the commentary on this privilege.

Along with the residential Bishops, titular Bishops when serving as Apostolic Administrators, and coadjutors of totally disabled Bishops enjoy the favor of this reservation.[15] For, as Roberti points out[16] the intention of canon 1557, § 2, 1° is to reserve to the competence of the Rota the contentious cases of anyone who functions as a ruler of a diocese. This reservation of forum is, likewise, enjoyed by Abbots and Prelates *nullius,* and by Vicars and Prefects Apostolic.[17] However, titular Bishops as such do not enjoy any special forum in contentious matters. In contentious cases they are subject to the local ecclesiastical tribunals in the same manner as priests and other minor clerics.[18]

Before the promulgation of the Code this reservation of the contentious cases of residential Bishops to the competence of the Rota

---

[11] Canon 1599, § 2.

[12] *Loc. cit.*

[13] Canon 1559, § 3.

[14] Roberti, *De Processibus,* I, n. 63, p. 187; Cappello, *Summa,* III, n. 14; Goyeneche, *De Processibus Breves Adnotationes ad L. IV Codicis Iuris Canonici, Vol. I De Iudiciis in Genere* (pro Manuscripto, Romae: ad S. Ioannis Lat.), p. 41 (hereafter cited *De Processibus*).

[15] Cappello, *Summa,* III, n. 27; Roberti, *De Processibus,* I, n. 63, p. 185.

[16] *Loc. cit.*

[17] Canons 215, § 2 and 249, § 1. Cf. Goyeneche, *De Processibus,* p. 41; Roberti, *De Processibus,* I, n. 63, p. 185; Coronata, *Institutiones,* III, n. 1097, *nota* 8.

[18] Vermeersch-Creusen, *Epitome,* III, n. 14; Cappello, *Summa,* III, n. 14; Roberti, *De Processibus,* p. 41.

did not exist. In fact, there was a dispute as to what judge was competent to hear them.[19] The Council of Trent (1545-1563) was silent about this matter, legislating only for the reservation of the major criminal cases of Bishops to the exclusive competence of the Roman Pontiff.[20]

Arguing from the silence of the Council of Trent, Barbosa (1589-1649),[21] claimed that the law previous to the Council of Trent remained in force,[22] and that the Metropolitan was competent to hear contentious cases which involved Bishops as defendants. However, if the Bishop was the plaintiff, Barbosa advised that the case be settled by arbiters or taken to the Sacred Congregations, since the Metropolitan enjoyed no jurisdiction over a defendant who was a subject of a suffragan Bishop. Reiffenstuel (1642-1703)[23] agreed with Barbosa on this question. Schmalzgrueber (1663-1735)[24] taught that the Metropolitan was competent to hear the contentious cases of his suffragan Bishops, no matter whether the Bishop was plaintiff or defendant.

Cardinal Petra (1662-1747)[26] whom Bouix (1808-1870)[27] and Wernz (1842-1914)[28] followed, taught that the Metropolitan or Archbishop was not competent to hear a contentious case in which a Bishop was involved either as a plaintiff or as a defendant. He denied the Archbishop's competence over contentious cases in which the Bishop was the plaintiff on the same grounds as Barbosa, namely, that the Archbishop enjoyed no jurisdiction over a defendant who was a subject of a suffragan Bishop. He denied the Arch-

---

[19] Petra, *Commentaria ad Constitutiones Apostolicas* (5 tom. in 2 vols., Venetiis: 1729), I, 159 (hereafter cited *Commentaria*); Bouix, *De Episcopo,* I, 458.

[20] Sess. XIII, *de ref.,* c. 6; cf. Schroeder, *Council of Trent,* p. 360; sess. XXIV, *de ref.,* c. 5; cf. Schroeder, *Council of Trent,* p. 466.

[21] *Iuris ecclesiastici universi libri III,* Vol. I, cap. VII, n. 46.

[22] Cf. cc. 9, 17 of Council of Chalcedon (451); cf. Schroeder, *Disciplinary Decrees,* pp. 98, 116; Thomassinus, Pars I, lib. I, cap. 10, n. 15.

[23] *Ius Canonicum Universum,* Lib. II, tit. 31, n. 38.

[24] *Ius Ecclesiasticum Universum,* Lib. I, tit. 31, n. 22; Lib. III, tit. 2, n. 74.

[26] *Commentaria,* I, 160 ff.

[27] *De Episcopo,* I, 457 ff.

[28] *Ius Decretalium,* V, n. 297.

bishop's competence when the Bishop was a defendant on the grounds of a reply of the Sacred Congregation of Bishops and Regulars as given on May 18, 1588,[29] which stated in effect that contentious cases which involved Bishops as defendants should be referred to the Roman Curia. This was probably the better warranted procedure, and seems to have been the procedure that was followed.

However, it is certain that before the Code the Rota did not enjoy competence for the first instance in the contentious trials of Bishops. Pope Pius X (1903-1914) in his Constitution *Sapienti consilio,*[30] restored the Rota to its former position as a tribunal of the Holy See. In the appendix to this Constitution were published the rules for the Rota. They made no mention of this tribunal's possession of competence over the contentious cases of Bishops.[31] The authors who before the Code commented on these rules insisted on the existence of the Rota as a tribunal of second instance only. They even mentioned that the cases of Bishops were not within the scope of the Rota's competence, unless these cases were submitted to the Rota *motu proprio* by the Roman Pontiff, or the parties in question requested a trial before the Rota.[32] The Code has, however, quite definitely established the competence of the Rota to hear in the first instance the contentious cases of residential Bishops.[33]

The privilege whereby the contentious cases of residential Bishops are reserved to the competence of the Rota, as has been clearly indicated, is new with the Code. But it is granted without prejudice to the special ruling enacted in canon 1572, § 2.[34] This canon rules that trials involving the temporal rights and goods of the Bishop, of the Bishop's mensal revenues and of the diocesan

---

[29] This reply itself was not available to the writer.

[30] 29 iun. 1908—*AAS,* I (1909), 1-20.

[31] *Lex Propria S. Romanae Rotae et Signaturae Apostolicae,* c. 15—*AAS,* I (1909), 24.

[32] Cf. Cappello, *De Curia Romana,* pp. 281-290; Monin, *De Curia Romana, ejus Historia ac Hodierna Disciplina iuxta Reformationem a Pio X Inductam* (Lovanii, 1912), pp. 343, 344.

[33] Canons 1557, § 2, 1° and 1599, § 2.

[34] Canon 1557, § 2. "Tribunalibus vero Sedis Apostolicae reservatur iudicare: 1° Episcopos residentiales in contentiosis, salvo praescripto can. 1572, § 2."

curia may be held, with the consent of the Bishop, before a diocesan tribunal sitting as a collegiate body composed of the *officialis* and two of the senior synodal judges. If the Bishop does not consent, these cases are to be tried before the immediate superior judge.[35]

Herein there seems to be a contradiction inasmuch as both canon 1557, § 2, 1°, and canon 1572, § 2, cover the same matter and apparently reserve the same contentious cases to different tribunals. For the wording of canon 1572, § 2, is general enough to include the cases covered by the reservation of canon 1557, § 2, 1°.[36]

Canon 1572, § 2, considers the temporal rights and goods of three distinct subjects, namely the Bishop, the Bishop's *mensa* and the diocesan curia.[37] There can be no doubt that contentious cases which involve the temporal rights and goods of the *mensa* and the diocesan curia[38] may be tried, with the consent of the Bishop, in a collegiate diocesan tribunal. For as separate subjects of rights and of the ownership of temporal goods, the *mensa* and the diocesan curia are not comprehended within the reservation of canon 1557, § 2, 1°.[39]

The problem arises when the temporal rights and goods of the Bishop are in litigation. Canon 1572, § 2, allows such litigation to be settled in a collegiate diocesan tribunal if the Bishop consents, or in the immediate superior tribunal if the Bishop refuses consent. Yet canon 1557, § 2, 1°, rules that such litigation be settled before the tribunals of the Holy See.

---

[35] Canon 1572, § 2. "Si vero agatur de iuribus aut bonis temporalibus Episcopi aut mensae vel Curiae dioecesanae, controversia dirimenda deferatur vel, Episcopo consentiente, ad dioecesanum tribunal collegiale quod constat officiali et duobus iudicibus synodalibus antiquioribus, vel ad iudicem immediate superiorem."

[36] Lega-Bartoccetti, *Commentarius in Iudicia,* I, 36; canon 1559, § 1.

[37] Roberti, *De Processibus,* I, n. 97, p. 259; Goyeneche, *De Processibus,* p. 67; Coronata, *Institutiones,* III, n. 1115.

[38] The goods of the *mensa* may be defined as the sum total of ecclesiastical revenues which supply the means of sustenance for the Bishop and his household. The goods of the diocesan curia may be defined as the sum total of revenues with which the Bishop supports those who aid him in the rule of the diocese, such as the *officialis,* the chancellor, etc.—Noval, *De Iudiciis,* p 59; Roberti, *ibid.,* p. 258.

[39] Roberti, *De Processibus,* I, n. 97, p. 259.

The first solution that was offered was that canon 1572, § 2, was concerned with contentious cases in which the Bishop appeared as plaintiff, while canon 1557, § 2, 1°, was concerned with the same case in which the Bishop appeared as defendant. This solution was rendered untenable by a reply of the Pontifical Commission for the Interpretation of the Code to the effect that a residential Bishop could both cite and be cited before a diocesan tribunal which was hearing a case that fell within the scope of canon 1572, § 2.[40]

In seeking a solution to this problem, Roberti[41] made reference to the preparatory schemata of the Code in which he noted that the preliminary draft of canon 1572, § 2, appeared under the title *"De foro competenti,"*[42] while in the final draft of the Code it appears without any change in its text under the title *"De tribunali ordinario primae instantiae."* From this he concluded that canon 1572, § 2, is concerned with the factor of competence, and that in virtue of this canon trials involving the temporal rights and goods of the residential Bishop may be held in the diocesan tribunal, provided that competence is duly established.

This explanation makes it clear that the diocesan collegiate tribunal enjoys competence over the cases mentioned, but it still does not seem to clear up the problem as to what cases are reserved to the Rota. Many authors[43] merely report the canons involved without offering any specific commentary. Lega-Bartoccetti[44] hold that personal cases in these matters are reserved to the Rota. Cappello[45] teaches that the private cases are reserved. The exact meaning of these authors is not clear. To the writer it seems that a distinction should be made for the proper understanding of the relationship of canon 1572, § 2, with canon 1557, § 2, 1°. In deal-

---

[40] PCI, 29 apr. 1940—*AAS,* XXXII (1940), 212.

[41] *De Processibus,* I, n. 97, p. 259.

[42] Roberti, *Codicis Iuris Canonici Schemata,* Lib. IV, *De Processibus,* I, *De Iudiciis in Genere* (in Civitate Vaticana: Typis Polyglottis Vaticanis, 1940), D, c. 11, § 2; E, c. 11, § 2; F, c. 5, § 1, 4°; G, c. 6, § 1, 4°.

[43] E.g., Vermeersch-Creusen, *Epitome,* III, nn. 14, 32; Regatillo, *Institutiones,* II, n. 345; Noval, *De Iudiciis,* p. 59; Coronata, *Institutiones,* III, nn. 1097, 1115.

[44] *Commentarius in Iudicia,* I, 36, 37, 110, 111.

[45] *Summa,* III, n. 14.

ing with the question of its own competence, the Sacred Roman Rota considered these canons and made a distinction between the Bishop as a subject of rights and property and the Bishop as a private person.[46] Using this distinction as a basis, the writer offers the following explanation. When the case is primarily concerned with the rights and property of the Bishop and only secondarily with the Bishop himself, the ruling of canon 1572, § 2, is to be followed. The trial, then, may be held before a collegiate tribunal of the diocese or the judiciary of the immediate superior court. When the case is primarily concerned with the Bishop and only secondarily with the Bishop's rights and property, canon 1557, § 2, 1° is to be followed. The trial in this latter case is to be held before the Rota. For example, if the case involved only the question of the Bishop's right to a certain property, the matter could be settled in a collegiate diocesan tribunal. If the case involved a Bishop on grounds of failure to fulfill a contract, the case would be reserved to the Rota for judicial settlement, since such a case would directly involve the person of the Bishop.[47] However, since in many cases it would be rather difficult to make such a distinction, it would be better to refer all such contentious cases to the Rota for adjudication.[48] Such a procedure is especially recommended in view of the fact that there is a possibility that a collegiate diocesan tribunal is absolutely incompetent,[49] and that its sentence thereby becomes vitiated with incurable nullity.[50]

Furthermore, to follow this procedure would not render canon 1572, § 2, ineffective. For that canon applies whether the Bishop

---

[46] S.R.R., *Damnorum,* 30 apr. 1923, coram R.P.D. Francisco Parillo, dec. IX, n. 4—*S. Romanae Rotae Decisiones seu Sententiae* (ab anno 1909, Romae: Typis Vaticanis, 1912-), XV (1923), 84, 85 (hereafter cited *Decisiones*). In this decision it should be noted that the Rota did not clearly explain the relationship existing between canon 1557, § 2, 1° and canon 1572, § 2.

[47] The Rota decided a similar case. Cf. S.R.R. *Crediti,* 22 iun. 1923, coram R.P.D. Francisco Salieri, Dec. XIII, n. 14—*Decisiones,* XV (1923), 124; *AAS,* XV (1923), pp. 515-517.

[48] Regatillo, *Institutiones,* II, n. 365.

[49] Canon 1558.

[50] Canon 1892, 1°.

be plaintiff or defendant.[51] It would certainly be applicable whenever the Bishop cites one of his own subjects as a defendant in a case involving the Bishop's rights or property, since the reservation of canon 1557, § 2, 1°, extends only to those contentious cases in which the Bishop is cited as defendant.[52]

The Rota enjoys no competence over residential Bishops in matters of diocesan administration and discipline. All recourse in these matters is to be taken to the Sacred Congregation of the Council.[53] If a cleric, for example, thinks that his rights were violated in consequence of a disciplinary decree of the residential Bishop, he must have recourse for the settlement of his grievance to the Sacred Congregation of the Council, which Congregation is also empowered to settle the question of damages if such a question be present.[54] The incompetence of the Rota in these matters is such that it may not hear any case which has its origin in administrative of disciplinary decrees of the residential Bishop, even if the case is concerned with damages desulting from such a disciplinary or administrative decree.[55]

---

[51] Lega-Bartoccetti, *Commentarius in Iudicia,* I, 36; Goyeneche, *De Processibus,* p. 67; PCI, 29 apr. 1940—*AAS,* XXXII (1940), 212.

[52] Cf. *supra,* p. 115.

[53] Canons 1601 and 250.

[54] Vermeersch-Creusen, *Epitome,* III, n. 4, 1; Goyeneche, *De Processibus,* p. 102.

[55] PCI, resp. 23 maii 1923—*AAS,* XVI (1924), 251; S.R.R., *Damnorum,* 30 apr. 1923, coram R.P.D. Francisco Parillo, Dec. IX, n. 2—*Decisiones,* XV (1923), 85; Coronata, *Institutiones,* III, n. 1136; Noval, *De Iudiciis,* n. 174, p. 101; Roberti, *De Processibus,* I, n. 132, p. 374.

CHAPTER VIII

PRIVILEGES ENJOYED BY RESIDENTIAL BISHOPS IN CONCEDING INDULGENCES IN THEIR DIOCESE

ARTICLE I. THE RESIDENTIAL BISHOP'S PRIVILEGE OF CONCEDING INDULGENCES IN HIS DIOCESES

An indulgence is a remission before God of all or of part of the temporal punishment due to sins whose guilt has already been forgiven. This remission is conceded by ecclesiastical authority from the treasury of the Church.[1] The infinite satisfaction of Our Saviour and the abundant satisfaction of the Blessed Virgin and of the Saints, make up this treasury, which is at the disposal of the Catholic Church.[2]

The power to grant indulgences, since it is an aspect of the power of the keys, requires jurisdiction for its exercise.[3] Universal jurisdiction over all ecclesiastical matters is enjoyed by the Roman Pontiff.[4] Consequently, the Pope alone exercises the primary and supreme power in granting indulgences.[5] No one other than the Pope may grant indulgences through ordinary power, except those to whom such power is expressly conceded by law.[6] Residential Bishops are among those who receive an express grant of this power from the law.[7]

The power of granting indulgences as enjoyed by residential Bishops is ordinary power for the reason that it is attached to their

---

[1] Canon 911.

[2] De Angelis, *De Indulgentiis,* nn. 5-8; Fanfani, *De Indulgentiis,* n. 1, pp. 2, 3.

[3] Fanfani, *De Indulgentiis,* n. 5; Coronata, *De Sacramentis,* II, n. 479.

[4] Canon 218.

[5] De Angelis, *De Indulgentiis,* n. 29; Cappello, *De Sacramentis,* II, n. 650.

[6] Canon 912.

[7] Canon 349, § 2. "A capta vero possessione Episcopi residentiales habent praeterea ius: 2° Concedendi indulgentias quinquaginta dierum in suae iurisdictionis locis; . . ."

office by law.[8] However, this fact does not derogate from the existence of this power as a privilege. For its exercise depends upon a special concession of the Holy See.[9] Thus it is a privilege, since a privilege is a concession of some special right made by a competent superior.[10]

Historically Bishops played an important part in the development of the doctrine of indulgences. It was through them that the earliest forms of indulgences were applied to the faithful in the form of the mitigation or termination of public penance.[11] During the ages of persecution, Christians doing public penance were wont to appeal to the martyrs for a mitigation of the severe penances to which they were subjected for their sins. The martyrs themselves did not attempt to relax their penances. Instead they furnished letters called *libelli pacis,* in which they pleaded for mercy for the bearer in view of their own sufferings for the Faith. The penitents in turn presented these letters to the Bishop, who on the strength of them usually remitted the public penance and admitted the bearer to communion with the Church.[12] St. Cyprian, Bishop of Carthage (+ 258),[13] and Tertullian (c. 160-c. 235)[14] testified to the existence of this practice.

It cannot, however, be held as certain that this practice was the equivalent of the granting of an indulgence as it is known today. For there exists the doubt whether or not the Church wished, at that time, in remitting public penance to grant from its treasury[15] a remission of temporal punishment. Nevertheless, this practice definitely shows that it was the Bishop who granted the mitigation

---

[8] Canons 349, § 2, 2° and 197, § 1.

[9] Wernz-Vidal, *Ius Canonicum,* Vol. IV, pars I, n. 155, *nota* 60.

[10] Roelker, *Principles of Privilege,* p. 16.

[11] Beringer, *Les Indulgences, Leur Nature et Leur Usage* (3. ed., Traduction par L'Abbé Ph. Mazoyer, 2 vols., Paris: P. Lethielleux, 1905), I, 39 (hereafter cited *Les Indulgences*).

[12] Morinus, *Commentarius Historicus de Disciplina in Administratione Sacramenti Poenitentiae lib. IX* (Venetiis, 1702), pp. 414 ff.

[13] *Epistola X (ad Martyres et Confessores) MPL,* IV, 256; *Epistola* XI *(ad Clerum de Lapsis)—MPL,* IV, 259.

[14] *De Pudicitia,* XXII—*MPL,* II, 1027.

[15] Beringer, *Les Indulgences,* I, n. 40; De Angelis, *De Indulgentiis,* n. 20.

of public penance. Councils of the fourth century[16] also point to the Bishop's power to lessen these public penances. Hence, in so far as the mitigation of public penance may be looked upon as an indulgence, it may be said with safety that Bishops granted the first indulgences.

It was not until the eleventh century that Bishops began to grant general indulgences. In about the year 1000, Bishop Ponce of Arles granted an indulgence that could be gained by all who kept a vigil in the Church of Mountmajor on the occasion of its consecration.[17] Bishop Anselm of Milan granted a similar indulgence in 1026 on the occasion of the consecration of the Church of the Holy Sepulcher.[18] Indulgences of this type were real indulgences[19] which were apparently granted by Bishops in their diocese without any particular expressed authorization of the Holy See.[20] For by the thirteenth century the IV General Council of the Lateran (1215) complained about the fact that Bishops were going to excess in granting indulgences, and accordingly limited their power in this matter to the granting of an indulgence of forty days.[21]

Though the Council of Trent (1545-1563) passed general legislation in the matter of indulgences,[22] it did not effect a change in the measure of the forty days' indulgence which was established by the IV Lateran Council[23] as within the power of Bishops to

---

[16] E.g., Council of Ancyra (314), c. 2—Mansi, II, 529; I General Council of Nicaea (325), c. 12—Schroeder, *Disciplinary Decrees*, p. 41.

[17] Lepicier, *Indulgences*, p. 289.

[18] Lepicier, *Indulgences*, p. 291.

[19] Cappello, *De Sacramentis*, II, n. 694.

[20] De Angelis, *De Indulgentiis*, nn. 21, 40.

[21] C. 62 ". . . ac deinde in anniversario dedicationis tempore quadraginta dies de injunctis poenitentiis indulta remissio non excedat. Hunc quoque dierum numerum indulgentiarum litteras praecipimus moderari, quae pro quibuslibet causis aliquoties conceduntur; cum Romanus Pontifex, qui plenitudinem obtinet potestatis hoc in talibus moderamen consueverit observare."—Schroeder, *Disciplinary Decrees*, p. 582 (c. 14, X, *de poenitentis et remissionibus*, V, 38).

[22] Sess, XXI, *de ref.*, c. 9—Schroeder, *Council of Trent*, p. 415; sess. XXV, *de ref.*, c. 21, *Decretum de Indulgentiis*—Schroeder, *Council of Trent*, pp. 518, 519.

[23] Cf. Fagnanus, *Commentaria*, in c. 14, X, *de poenitentis et remissionibus*, V, 38, nn. 14, 15.

grant. In fact, this measure remained unchanged until 1903.[24] In that year Pope Pius X (1903-1914) increased the measure to fifty days in favor of all residential Bishops,[25] and this measure was restated by the Code.[26] It remained unchanged until it was doubled in 1942 by Pope Pius XII on the occasion of the twenty-fifth anniversary of his elevation to the Episcopate.[27] Today, then, residential Bishops may grant an indulgence of 100 days in places subject to their jurisdiction (*in suae iurisdictione locis*).

When residential Bishops grant a general indulgence of 100 days in their diocese, it may be gained by all the faithful who are actually within the limits of the diocese. It may also be gained by the Bishop's subjects outide the diocese.[28] This, of course, is to be understood of indulgences that are not merely local, i.e., attached to some particular place, such as a church. For local indulgences may not be gained outside of the place to which they are attached.[29]

A reply of the Pontifical Commission for the Interpretation of the Code[30] makes it certain that exempt religious may gain indulgences granted by residential Bishops. This reply amounts to a restatement by the Commission of canon 927 as far as the exempt religious themselves are concerned, since the canon itself mentions them as among those capable of gaining Episcopal indulgences.[31] However, the reply does not establish as certain the Bishop's right to grant indulgences in exempt churches as well as in the monasteries and convents of Regulars.[32]

---

[24] Vives, *De Dignitate Episcoporum*, n. 2017; Wernz-Vidal, *Ius Canonicum*, Vol. IV, pars I, n. 155, *nota* 61.

[25] S.C. Indulg., *Urbis et Orbis*, 28 aug. 1903—*ASS*, XXXVI (1903-1904), 319.

[26] Canon 349, § 2, 2°.

[27] S. Poenit., decr. 20 iul. 1942—*AAS*, XXXIV (1942), 240.

[28] Canon 927.

[29] De Angelis, *De Indulgentiis*, n. 45.

[30] 6 dec. 1930—*AAS*, XXIII (1931), 25.

[31] Larraona, "Adnotationes"—*Commentarium pro Religiosis* (Romae, 1920- ; ab anno 1935, *Commentarium pro Religiosis et Missionariis*), XII (1931), 11, 12 (hereafter cited *Commentarium*).

[32] Vermeersch, "De Locis in Quibus Episcopi Indulgentias Concedere Possunt"—*Periodica*, XIX (1930), 25*, 26*.

In attaching indulgences to printed copies of prayers which will certainly circulate outside of their diocese, residential Bishops should keep in mind canon 925, § 1, which requires that the one gaining the indulgence be a subject of the grantor. Since the faithful can not be expected to know of this requirement, it would be prudent for the Bishop to note on such copies of prayers that the indulgences annexed thereto may be gained by the faithful of diocese X.[33]

Though it is through ordinary power that residential Bishops grant indulgences, they may not delegate this faculty. Canon 913, 1°, expressly states that the faculty of granting indulgences enjoyed by one of a rank inferior to the Roman Pontiff cannot be committed to others, unless express permission to do so has been granted by the Holy See. This prevents the Vicar General from granting indulgences even with a special mandate of the Bishop.[34]

Other limitations are placed on this Episcopal faculty. Residential Bishops may not grant indulgences applicable to the souls in purgatory.[35] They may not enrich with additional indulgences the same pious objects, works of piety, or membership in societies that have already been indulgenced by the Roman Pontiff or another Prelate. They may, however, grant additional indulgences, provided that they prescribe new conditions for the gaining of the same, e.g., additional prayers or other good works.[36]

Since the granting of an indulgence is an act of jurisdiction, residential Bishops may grant indulgences as soon as they have taken canonical possession of their diocese, even though they are not as yet consecrated.[37] The same faculty is enjoyed by titular

---

[33] Mutch, "Episcopal Indulgences"—*The Homiletic and Pastoral Review,* XLVII (1947), 216, 217. The indulgence could be gained by all who would recite these prayers within the limits of the diocese of the grantor, even though they were not his subjects. Cf. canon 927.

[34] Cappello, *De Sacramentis,* II, n. 651, 4°; Coronata, *De Sacramentis,* I, n. 479; De Angelis, *De Indulgentiis,* n. 42; Fanfani, *De Indulgentiis,* n. 9.

[35] Canon 913, 2°.

[36] Canon 913, 3°, Coronata, *De Sacramentis,* I, n. 480.

[37] Wernz-Vidal, *Ius Canonicum,* Vol. IV, pars I, n. 155; Coronata, *De Sacramentis,* I, n. 479.

Bishops serving as permanent Apostolic Administrators[38] and by the Coadjutors of totally disabled Bishops.[39] Moreover, Vicars and Prefects Apostolic during their term of office may also grant an indulgence of 100 days in the territory subject to them, even though they lack Episcopal consecration.[40] Abbots and Prelates *nullius* enjoy this same faculty of granting an indulgence of 100 days.[41]

Titular Bishops as such, however, may not grant indulgences in any diocese.[42]

In conclusion, one may summarize as follows the extent of the Bishop's privilege of granting indulgences: residential Bishops and titular Bishops serving as permanent Apostolic Administrators or as Coadjutors of totally disabled Bishops may grant an indulgence of 100 days anywhere within the physical limits of their diocese. The indulgence itself may be gained by their subjects while outside the diocese, by a visitor to the diocese with a domicile elsewhere, and by those in the diocese who have no domicile whatsoever, as well as by exempt religious sojourning in the diocese, unless the terms of the concession exclude such persons.

ARTICLE II. THE PRIVILEGE OF GRANTING THE PAPAL BLESSING WITH A PLENARY INDULGENCE

Before the occupation of Rome in 1870, the Roman Pontiffs were accustomed to bestow a solemn blessing and impart a plenary

---

[38] Canon 315, § 1, grants permanent Apostolic Administrators the same power that is granted to the residential Bishops. Hence they may grant indulgences. Cf. McDonough, *Apostolic Administrators*, pp. 162, 163.

[39] Canon 351, § 2, implies that the Coadjutor of a totally disabled Bishop assumes all the power of the residential Bishop. On the strength of this there seems to be no doubt that these Coadjutors can grant indulgences. However the letter of their appointment may provide otherwise. Cf. Lynch, *Coadjutors*, p. 77.

[40] Canon 294, § 2; S. Poenit., *decr.* 20 iul. 1942—*AAS*, XXXIV (1942), 240; De Angelis, *De Indulgentiis*, n. 47; Vermeersch-Creusen, *Epitome*, II, n. 204.

[41] Canon 323, § 1; S. Poenit., *decr. cit.;* De Angelis, *De Indulgentiis*, nn. 50, 51; Cappello, *De Sacramentis*, II, n. 651; Fanfani, *De Indulgentiis*, n. 9.

[42] S.C. Indulg., resp. 12 ian. 1878, ad 4—*Decr. Auth. S.C. Indulg.*, n. 433; De Angelis, *De Indulgentiis*, n. 45, a, b; Coronata, *De Sacramentis*, I, n. 479.

indulgence on Holy Thursday and Easter (at St. Peter's), on the Feast of the Ascension (at the Lateran), and on the Feast of the Assumption (at St. Mary Major's). These blessings were intended for the whole world.[43] But since the number of the faithful who could be present on such occasions was necessarily small, the Roman Pontiffs frequently delegated to others the privilege of giving the blessing in the Pontiff's name and of granting the plenary indulgence attached thereto.[44]

On September 3, 1762, Pope Clement XIII (1758-1769)[45] revoked all previous privileges granted to individuals, and empowered Patriarchs, Primates, Archbishops and Bishops to bestow this blessing with the annexed plenary indulgence twice a year, once on Easter Sunday, and again on one of the principal feasts of the year to be selected by each of these. This grant of Clement XIII is incorporated in the Code.[46] Pope Pius XII in 1942 increased this grant, so that now the papal blessing with the annexed plenary indulgence may be imparted three times a year.[47]

The days on which the papal blessing may be imparted are Easter and two other more solemn feasts of the year to be designated by the residential Bishop.[48]

The more solemn feasts of the year are at least those mentioned in the *Bishop's Ceremonial.*[49] They are the Nativity, the Epiphany, Holy Thursday, the Ascension, also the Feasts of the Immaculate Conception, of the Annunciation and of the Assumption of the Blessed Virgin, as well as the feasts of St. Joseph, of the Apostles

---

[43] Beringer, *Les Indulgences,* II, n. 305, p. 189.

[44] St. Charles Borromeo (1538-1584) enjoyed such a privilege. Cf. Catalanus, *Caeremoniale Episcoporum,* I, 25, sub § 1.

[45] Const. *Inexhaustum—Fontes,* n. 451.

[46] Canon 914.—"Benedictionem papalem cum indulgentia plenaria, secundum praescriptam formulam, impertiri possunt Episcopi in sua quisque dioecesi bis in anno, hoc est die sollemni Paschatis Resurrectionis et alio die festo sollemni ab ipsis designando, etiamsi iidem Missae sollemni adstiterint tantum; . . ."

[47] S. Poenit., *decr.* 20 iul. 1940—*AAS,* XXXIV (1942), 240; Bouscaren, *Digest,* II, 221.

[48] Canon 914; S. Poenit., *decr. cit.*

[49] Lib. II, cap. XXXIV, n. 2.

Peter and Paul, of All Saints, and of the Titular of the Church.[50] The Bishop should choose any two of these feasts for imparting the papal blessing.[51]

On the feasts selected the residential Bishop himself must impart the blessing at the end of the Solemn Mass.[52] There is no longer any need that the Bishop celebrate the Mass. It is sufficient that he assist at the Mass.[53] Nor is the Bishop restricted if he lacks a reason for not celebrating,[54] as was formerly the case.[55] He may impart the blessing provided that he assist at the Solemn Mass, and he himself may gain the plenary indulgence annexed thereto.[56]

This blessing may be imparted by a residential Bishop in any church of his diocese.[57]

A Bishop who is ruling over more than one diocese may not, on his own authority, transfer to another day in one of his dioceses the papal blessing annexed to Easter Sunday.[58] However, this regulation would not seem to prevent a Bishop who rules two dioceses from giving the papal blessing in both dioceses on Easter Sunday if this be physically possible. This interpretation fits in well with the present law which allows the Bishop to impart the blessing when assisting at Solemn Mass. As for the second and third occasions on which this blessing is to be imparted, the Bishop may select different days in the two dioceses, since canon 914 does not determine specific days for the imparting of the blessing and the plenary indulgence. In this way it is possible for a Bishop who rules two dioceses to impart the papal blessing three times in each.[59]

---

[50] Cf. Moretti, *De Sacris Functionibus,* I, nn. 78, 118.

[51] Blat, *Commentarium,* Lib. III, pars I, p. 300.

[52] Moretti, *De Sacris Functionibus,* II, n. 968, 1.

[53] Canon 914.

[54] Wernz-Vidal, *Ius Canonicum,* Vol. IV, pars I, n. 163; Coronata, *De Sacramentis,* I, n. 483.

[55] S.R.C., resp. 15 ian. 1847—*Decr. Auth.,* n. 2925; Vives, *De Dignitate Episcoporum,* n. 1131.

[56] S.C. Indulg., resp. 20 maii 1896—*ASS,* XXVIII (1895-1896), 750; De Angelis, *De Indulgentiis,* n. 146.

[57] Canon 914; Coronata, *De Sacramentis,* I, n. 483.

[58] PCI, resp. 17 febr. 1930—*AAS,* XXII (1930), 195.

[59] De Angelis, *De Indulgentiis,* n. 152.

The faculty of imparting the papal blessing may not be delegated to anyone.[60]

When the Bishop imparts the papal blessing he must use the formula originally given in the Constitution *Inexhaustum* of Pope Clement XIII,[61] now contained in the *Roman Pontifical.*[62] The formula is of obligation and must be followed.[63] After the last gospel of the Mass, the Bishop sits on the throne or faldstool while the Pontifical Brief by which power is given to the Bishop to bestow the papal blessing is read both in Latin and in the vernacular.[64] Then upon rising the Bishop recites the preliminary prayers, and on receiving the miter and crozier he imparts the blessing with a triple sign of the cross with the usual words, *"et benedictio Dei omnipotentis, Pa + tris, et Fi + lii, et Spiritus + Sancti descendat super vos et maneat semper.* (R) *Amen.* At the conclusion of this the Bishop remains at the throne or faldstool while the formula of the indulgence is read both in Latin and in the vernacular.[65]

ARTICLE III. THE PRIVILEGE OF ESTABLISHING DAILY AND PERPETUALLY PRIVILEGED ALTARS

A privileged altar is one to which is attached a plenary indulgence applicable to the one for whom the Mass is offered.[66] There

---

[60] Canon 913, 1°; S. Poenit., resp. (private), 25 apr. 1922—Bouscaren, *Digest,* I, 419. This response is not published in the *AAS.*

[61] 3 sept. 1762—*Fontes,* n. 451.

[62] *Pontificale Romanum,* Appendix, Ritus et Formula Benedictionis Apostolicae.

[63] Melata, "De Benedictione Papale eiusque Ritu Servando"—*Analecta Ecclesiastica,* III (1895), 38; Beringer, *Les Indulgences,* II, n. 50, p. 34.

[64] The Sacred Congregation of Rites is not willing to dispense from the reading of the Brief both in Latin and in the vernacular. Cf. resp., 7 dec. 1844—*Decr. Auth.,* n. 2871.

[65] *Pontificale Romanum,* Appendix, Ritus et Formula Benedictionis Apostolicae; *Caeremoniale Episcoporum,* Lib. I, cap. XXV, nn. 1-8; Moretti, *De Sacris Functionibus,* II, nn. 968-970.

[66] The privileged altar, the extent of the privilege and the regulations for its use have already been discussed, and will not again be treated here. Cf. *supra,* pp. ?.

were a few examples of privileged altars as early as 1537.[67] Pope Benedict XIII (1724-1730)[68] was the first Pontiff to grant a general favor whereby Bishops and other Prelates could designate as privileged one altar in their patriarchial, metropolitan and cathedral churches. Later, Pope Clement XIII (1758-1769) empowered Bishops to designate a privileged altar in each of their parish churches. However, this designation had to be renewed every seven years.[69] The Code has repealed this formality of renewal, and confers upon Bishops, Abbots and Prelates *nullius,* Vicars and Prefects Apostolic, and the Major Superiors of clerical exempt religious institutes, the faculty of designating one altar as daily and perpetually privileged in their cathedral and abbatial churches, in collegiate and conventual churches, and in parish and quasi-parish churches. This faculty cannot be exercised in favor of public or semi-public oratories, unless these oratories serve as subsidiary churches to the parish churches.[70]

The altar which the Bishops designate as privileged must be a fixed or immovable altar, in the sense that it is considered to be the permanent altar in the church. The emphasis is on the permanence of the altar in the church not on the liturgical requirements for a permanent altar, that is, that the table and supports forming one unit are consecrated together.[71] The altars so common in many American churches, namely, those which are certainly permanent as to the church building itself but not as to liturgical requirements for permanence, can surely be designated

[67] Ferraris, *Prompta Bibliotheca,* s.v. "altare privilegiatum," nn. 19, 27.

[68] Const. *Omnium salute,* 20 aug. 1724—*Bull Rom.,* XXII, 76.

[69] S.C. Indulg., *Urbis et Orbis,* 19 maii 1759—*Fontes,* n. 4983.

[70] Canon 916.—"Episcopi, Abbates vel Praelati *nullius,* Vicarii ac Praefecti Apostolici et Superiores maiores religionis clericalis exemptae, possunt designare et declarare unum altare privilegiatum quotidianum perpetuum, dummodo aliud non habeatur, in suis ecclesiis cathedralibus, abbatialibus, collegiatis, conventualibus, paroecialibus, quasi-paroecialibus, non autem in oratoriis publicis vel semi-publicis, nisi sint ecclesiae paroeciali unita seu eiusdem subsidiaria."

[71] S.C. Indulg., resp. 15 dec. 1841, ad 3—*Decr. Auth. S.C. Indulg.,* n. 295; resp. 18 iul. 1902, ad 2—*ASS,* XXXV (1902-1903), 62; Many, *De Locis Sacris,* n. 134; De Meester, *Compendium,* Tom III, pars I, n. 1161; Vermeersch-Creusen, *Epitome,* II, n. 211; De Angelis, *De Indulgentiis,* n. 307.

as privileged altars. Beyond this, the altar may be constructed of wood except for the consecrated altar stone.[72] The privilege itself, however, is not attached to the altar stone but to the altar, in so far as it is dedicated to the honor of God or of His saints.[73] Thus the changing of the altar stone would not affect the privileged status of the altar itself.[74] It should further be noted that the churches in which Bishops designate such privileged altars need not be consecrated. It is sufficient that they be blessed.[75]

Aside from the consideration of the altar, canon 916 places the condition, "provided that there is not another privileged altar in the church" (*dummodo aliud non habeatur*). To understand the extent of this condition it is necessary to go back to the Constitution *Inexhaustum* of Pope Clement XIII, from which it is clear that the favored altars were to be privileged for all the faithful.

The authors[76] interpret this condition in the light of the Constitution to mean "provided that there is not another altar in the church privileged for all the faithful." Hence, if in a church there were an altar even daily and perpetually privileged for the members of a confraternity or a sodality, the Bishop could declare another altar in that same church daily and perpetually privileged for all the faithful. But should there be in the church an altar privileged for all the faithful, even though privileged for only seven years, the Bishop could not designate another altar as daily and perpetually privileged in that church. In this case the Bishop's power is suspended until there has elapsed the period of time for which the already favored altar was privileged. Then the Bishop could designate it or another altar as daily and perpetually privileged. For the essence of this privilege is not the time element but the desire that the altar be privileged for all the faithful.[77]

---

[72] S.C. Indulg., resp. 18 iul. 1902, ad 3—*ASS*, XXXV (1902-1903), 62.

[73] S.C. Indulg., resp. 27 sept. 1843—*Decr. Auth. S.C. Indulg.*, n. 324.

[74] Coronata, *De Sacramentis*, I, n. 489; De Angelis, *De Indulgentiis*, n. 307.

[75] S.C. Indulg., resp. 30 ian. 1760, ad 2—*Decr. Auth. S.C. Indulg.*, n. 219.

[76] Regatillo, *Ius Sacramentarium*, I, n. 705; Blat, *Commentarium*, Lib. III, pars I, p. 300; De Angelis, *De Indulgentiis*, n. 310; Coronata, *De Sacramentis*, I, n. 490.

[77] De Angelis, *De Indulgentiis*, n. 309; Coronata, *De Sacramentis*, I, n. 940.

Even if a cathedral serves as a parish church, it may not on this account enjoy two altars privileged for all the faithful.[78]

Canon 916 mentions that the residential Bishop may not use this faculty in public or semi-public oratories unless these oratories are used as subsidiary or filial churches. A filial church is one in which parochial functions such as funeral services and the administration of Baptism and the Holy Eucharist take place. In such oratories a privileged altar may be designated.[79]

The privileged status should be indicated on the altar with the following inscription, *"Altare privilegiatum, quotidianum et perpetuum."*[80] Further, a record should be kept of the designation of each privileged altar. The following formula is suggested for this record.

N. N.

Dei et Apostolicae Sedis gratia Episcopus . . .

Decretum

Attentis a dilecto filio . . . expositis, Nos, eius preces libenter excipientes, facultate nostra ordinaria declaramus privilegiatum quotidianum Altare tit. . . . in ecclesia paroeciali . . . (vel cathedrali) loci . . . intra fines dioecesis nostrae, in favorem animae alicuius christifidelis in Dei gratia vita functi, in cuius suffragium ibi Missa a quocumque Sacerdote celebrabitur, dummodo in ipsa ecclesia aliud Altare eodem privilegio iam decoratum non habeatur.

Datem . . . ex nostris Aedibus, die . . . anno . . .

L. + S.

N. N. Episcopus[81]

---

[78] S.C. Indulg., resp. 10 sept. 1781—*Decr. Auth. S.C. Indulg.*, n. 241; Coronata, *De Sacramentis*, I, n. 490; Augustine, *Commentary*, IV, 367; De Angelis, *De Indulgentiis*, n. 312.

[79] S.C. Indulg., resp. 27 nov. 1764, ad 2—*Decr. Auth. S.C. Indulg.*, n. 234; Coronata, *De Sacramentis*, I, n. 490; De Angelis, *De Indulgentiis*, n. 314.

[80] Canon 918, § 1.

[81] Cf. De Angelis, *De Indulgentiis*, Appendix, V, n. 1.

No ceremony is designated for the establishment of these permanently privileged altars. The mere sending of the decree establishes any altar as permanently privileged. A further concluding note should remind Bishops Ordinaries that they may not delegate this faculty even to their Vicar Generals unless they enjoy an expressed indult of the Holy See that would allow such delegation.[82]

[82] S.C. Indulg., resp. 24 maii 1843—*Decr. Auth. S.C. Indulg.*, n. 322: canon 913, 1°; De Angelis, *De Indulgentiis*, n. 314.

CHAPTER IX

Miscellaneous Privileges of Residential Bishops

Article I. The Residential Bishop's Privilege of Precedence within His Own Diocese

Precedence may be defined as the right marshalling of people according to their rank, office, seniority or dignity for the purpose of giving to each by position the honor that is due to him.[1]

The general norms of precedence prescribe that those who have authority over others take precedence over them.[2] A residential Bishop, then, who takes precedence over his subjects within his diocese does so not by privilege but by right. But canon 347 further prescribes that the residential Bishop within the limits of his diocese precedes all Archbishops and Bishops with the exception of Cardinals, Papal Legates and the Bishop's own Metropolitan.[3]

Here it is stated that the residential Bishop takes the place of honor by privilege. For the general norms provide for another arrangement. Persons of a higher rank are to precede those of an inferior rank. Persons of the same rank but of a different order have precedence according to a higher or inferior order.[4] Persons of the same rank and degree of order take precedence according to the order of time in which they were elevated to the rank or order.[5]

The privilege consists in this. The residential Bishop enjoys the place of honor in his diocese even though there be present Prelates of higher rank or of senior elevation to the Episcopate.

---

[1] Regatillo, *Institutiones,* I, n. 215; Beste, *Introductio,* p. 162.

[2] Canon 106, 2°.

[3] Canon 347, "In suo territorio Episcopus praecedit omnibus Archiepiscopis et Episcopis, exceptis Cardinalibus, Legatis Pontificiis et proprio Metropolita; extra territorium serventur normae traditae in can. 106."

[4] Rank has reference to the hierarchical degree of jurisdiction. Order means the same as ordination in the various degrees of the hierarchy of Orders. Woywod, *Commentary,* I, 47.

[5] Canon 106, 3°.

In substance this privilege is not new. Local councils from the fourth century onward legislated that the place of honor was to be reserved for the Bishop in his diocese.[6] The problem of precedence really came to the fore in the greater assemblies of the clergy. Many disputes on precedence arose between Cardinals and Bishops.[7]

Until the eleventh century, Bishops enjoyed precedence over Cardinals. Official documents of the period support this fact. For example, the Constitution *Cum conventus* of Pope John XV (993)[8] was signed by four Bishops before the name of Cardinal Bonizo, Archpriest of St. Lucia (+ ca. 1090), appeared on it. But in the eleventh century Cardinals began to assume a position of preeminence in the Church when they became more closely united with the Pope in the administration of the Church.[9] This factor naturally affected the norms determining precedence, with the result that by the thirteenth century Cardinals were taking precedence over Bishops in most of the public assemblies.[10] In 1439 Pope Eugene IV (1431-1447) established definitely the precedence of Cardinals over Bishops and other Prelates.[11]

After the question of the Cardinal's precedence over Bishop's was settled by Pope Eugene IV, the present law on the Bishop's precedence within his diocese began to appear in replies of the Sacred Congregation of Rites.[12] These replies stated, as the Code does, that the residential Bishop enjoyed precedence over all

---

[6] E.g., Council of Laodicea (343-381), c. 56—Bruns, I, 79 (c. 8, D. XCV); Council of Carthage (401), c. 35—Bruns, I, 45 (c. 10, D. XCV); II Council of Braga (563), c. 6—Bruns, II, 34 (c. 1, D. XVIII); IV Council of Toledo (633), c. 4—Bruns, I, 222.

[7] Petra, *Commentaria,* I, 78 ff.

[8] *Bull. Rom.,* I, 460; Jaffé, n. 3848.

[9] Pope Nicholas II in 1059 gave Cardinals a predominant role in the election of the Roman Pontiff.—c. 1, D. XXIII; Benedictus XIV, *De Synodo Dioecesana* (2. Parmensis ed., 2 vols., Parmae, 1764), I, 65.

[10] Cardinals preceded Bishops at the I (1245) and II (1274) General Councils of Lyons; cf. Benedictus XIV, *loc. cit.;* Hardouin, VII, 670.

[11] Ep. *Non mediocri—Fontes,* n. 50.

[12] E.g., *Barcinonen,* 10 ian. 1609—*Fontes,* n. 5246; *Ephesina,* 8 apr. 1656—*Fontes,* n. 5485. For a fuller listing of these replies the reader is referred to Vives, *De Dignitate Episcoporum,* nn. 1434-1446.

Bishops and Archbishops, with the exception of Cardinals, Papal Legates and their own Metropolitans. The Council of Trent (1545-1563) had stated previously to these replies that each Bishop was to receive the honor in keeping with his dignity. He was to have the first place in choir, in processions and in other public functions.[13] The replies then appear to be an interpretation of this statement of the Council of Trent. The same replies were promulgated in law for the entire Church by Popes Innocent XIII (1721-1724)[14] and Benedict XIII (1724-1730),[15] and in turn served as the basis of the present law of the Code.

The law of the Code makes it clear that the residential Bishop in his diocese may precede all Bishops and Archbishops with the exception of Cardinals, Papal Legates and his own Metropolitan. However, the law is not clear with regard to Patriarchs and Primates. There can be raised the question whether or not the residential Bishop in his diocese precedes these Prelates. The authors are not in agreement on an answer. Some authors do not consider this question specifically.[16] Blat[17] claims that Patriarchs and Primates are not comprehended under the term "Archbishops" of canon 347, and therefore the question of their precedence is to be settled according to the norm of canon 280,[18] which rules that Patriarchs precede Primates, Primates precede Archbishops, and Archbishops precede Bishops, with all due observance being accorded to the rule mentioned in canon 347. In considering the phrase of canon 280 which adverts to the special ruling contained in canon 347, Blat argues that the position of the comma before the words *"hic Episcopis"* in canon 280 indicates that the phrase is limited in its application to Archbishops, and that in consequence of this Patriarchs and Primates precede the residential Bishop in his own diocese.

---

[13] Sess. XXV, *de ref.*, c. 6; Schroeder, *Council of Trent,* p. 505.

[14] Const. *Apostolici ministerii,* 23 maii 1723, § 15—*Fontes,* n. 280.

[15] Const. *In supremo,* 23 sept. 1724, § 12—*Fontes,* n. 283.

[16] E.g., Chelodi, *Ius de Personis,* n. 195, p. 320; Wernz-Vidal, *Ius Canonicum,* II, n. 599, p. 752; De Meester, *Compendium,* II, n. 207.

[17] *Commentarium,* II, n. 375.

[18] "Patriarcha praecedit Primati, Primas Archiepiscopo, hic Episcopis, salvo praescripto can. 347."

On the other hand, Cappello,[19] Coronata[20] and Vermeersch-Creusen[21] interpret both canon 280 and canon 347 to mean that the residential Bishop in his diocese precedes Patriarchs and Primates. Toso[22] limits the residential Bishop's precedence in this circumstance to the privilege of preceding only Latin Patriarchs and Primates.

Of the opinions proposed, the writer readily accepts Blat's opinion that the question of the residential Bishop's precedence over Patriarchs and Primates is to be settled according to canon 280, but he does not agree to Blat's interpretation of it. For it appears that the commas as used in canon 280 are employed not to limit the application of the phrase *"salvo praescripto can. 347,"* but merely to set off each fact as stated in the canon, so that the phrase in question would be regarded as applying to the entire canon with the consequence that the residential Bishop in his diocese should be regarded as entitled to precede Patriarchs and Primates.

The limitation of the privilege to precedence over Latin Patriarchs and Primates as proposed by Toso seems to be without foundation, since canon 106, 4°, rules that the question of rite does not enter into the determination of precedence. In view of this, the writer maintains that in consequence of the norms enacted in canons 347 and 280 the residential Bishop in his diocese precedes all Patriarchs, Primates, whether Latin or Oriental, and all Archbishops and Bishops, with the exception of Cardinals, Papal Legates and his own Metropolitan.

It should be noted that on the grounds of courtesy the residential Bishop may give his place of honor to a visiting Prelate.[23]

Outside his diocese a residential Bishop follows the general norms of precedence. He precedes all those who are inferior to him in rank and orders. Among those of the same rank and order, his precedence will be determined according to the time of appoint-

---

[19] *Summa,* I, n. 386.

[20] *Institutiones,* I, n. 365, 4°.

[21] *Epitome,* I, n. 393.

[22] *Commentaria,* Lib. II, tom. II, p. 178.

[23] S.R.C., decr. 12 iun. 1899—*Decr. Auth.,* n. 4023; resp. 26 nov. 1919, ad V, n. 3—*AAS,* XII (1920), 178.

ment or, if the date of appointment is the same, by the time of ordination.[24]

ARTICLE II. THE RESIDENTIAL BISHOP'S PRIVILEGE OF BEING NAMED IN THE CANON OF THE MASS

Liturgical laws give residential Bishops the privilege of having their name mentioned in the Canon of every Mass celebrated in their diocese even in Masses celebrated by exempt religious.[25] The Bishop is entitled to this mention from the day on which he takes possession of his See.[26] However, all Bishops, residential or titular, use the words *"et me indigno servo tuo"* in place of the words *"et antistite nostro 'N'"* of the Canon of the Mass.[27]

Further analogous privileges are conferred on residential Bishops by liturgical law. In all Masses celebrated in the diocese, a commemoration for the Bishop is to be made on the anniversary day of the latter's appointment to the diocese.[28] This anniversary is to be computed from the day on which the Bishop was appointed in the Sacred Consistorial Congregation.[29]

Likewise, the residential Bishop is to be named in the Divine Office in the ferial prayers (*preces feriales*) of Lauds and Vespers.[30] However, all Bishops may omit in these ferial prayers the versicle *"Oremus pro antistite nostro 'N'"* together with its response.[31]

The Coadjutor of a totally incapacitated Bishop does not enjoy these privileges. For there is only one principal Bishop in a diocese, in this case the residential Bishop. As long as he continues to be the principal Bishop he has the exclusive right to be mentioned in all these prayers and commemorations, as he alone holds the

[24] Canons 347 and 106, 3°.

[25] *Missale Romanum,* Ritus servandus in celebratione Missae, VII, 2; Moretti, *De Sacris Functionibus,* I, n. 77 (2).

[26] S.R.C., resp. 4 iul. 1879, ad 2—*Decr. Auth.,* n. 3500.

[27] *Missale Romanum, loc. cit.;* Moretti, *De Sacris Functionibus,* I, n. 76 (4).

[28] *Caeremoniale Episcoporum,* Lib. II, cap. XXXV.

[29] S.R.C., *Urbis et Orbis,* 8 iun. 1910—*AAS,* II (1910), 486; *Urbis et Orbis,* 8 iul. 1910—*AAS,* II (1910), 552, 553.

[30] Moretti, *De Sacris Functionibus,* I, n. 77 (2).

[31] Moretti, *ibid.,* n. 76 (4).

Episcopal benefice. The Sacred Congregation of Rites replied to this effect in reference to the Coadjutor of the Archdiocese of Pisa.[32] The permanent Apostolic Administrator, since he is equal to the residential Bishop in all things,[33] is entitled to mention in the Canon of the Mass and in the ferial prayers of Lauds and Vespers, as well as to a commemoration at Mass on the anniversary day of his appointment to the diocese.[34]

The present writer's reason for treating two practically identical offices in opposite fashion is this. The Coadjutor as here considered substitutes for a residential Bishop who actually remains in office. Hence, he is not entitled to the latter's privileges of liturgical commemoration. The Apostolic Administrator, on the other hand, is not in strict terminology simply a substitute. He actually holds the office of ruler of the diocese,[35] and thus is entitled to these privileges.

ARTICLE III. THE RESIDENTIAL BISHOP'S PRIVILEGE OF BURIAL WITHIN A CHURCH

The present law forbids the burial of the faithful within a church. But it allows the mortal remains of residential Bishops and of Abbots and Prelates *nullius,* to be interred within their churches.[36]

The interment of Bishops within the precincts of a church is of early origin. Eusebius (ca. 263-339)[37] mentioned that it was allowed in the time of the Emperor Justinian (527-566). Many (+ 1922)[38] stated that it was always expected that a Bishop would be buried within the confines of his cathedral. This, he stated, was evident from the *Bishops' Ceremonial,*[39] which supposes that every

---

[32] S.R.C., *Pisana,* 11 mart. 1882—*Decr. Auth.,* n. 3538. Cf. Lynch, *Coadjutors,* p. 78.

[33] Canon 315, § 1; Vermeersch-Creusen, *Epitome,* I, n. 433.

[34] McDonough, *Apostolic Administrators,* p. 164.

[35] Canon 312.

[36] Canon 1205, § 2.—"In ecclesiis cadavera ne sepeliantur, nisi agatur de cadaveribus Episcoporum residentialium, Abbatum vel Praelatorum *nullius* in propria ecclesia sepeliendis, vel Romani Pontificis, regalium personarum aut S.R.E. Cardinalium."

[37] *Historia Ecclesiastica,* Lib. IV, cap. XLV—*MPG,* LXVII, 836.

[38] *De Locis Sacris,* n. 174.

[39] Lib. II, cap. XXXVIII.

detail of the Bishop's funeral is to be carried out within the precincts of the church. However, before the Code this privilege was not exclusively episcopal. Canon 52 of the Council of Mainz (813),[40] which appears in Gratian's Collection,[41] seemed to be aimed at limiting interment within a church to Bishops and other outstanding persons. But, as Schmalzgrueber[42] pointed out, this regulation was interpreted in such a way that anyone of the faithful could be interred within a church. Ferraris (+ ca. 1763)[43] stated that this same practice was still followed in the early eighteenth century.

The use of this right of burial within the church is not obligatory on the residential Bishop.[44] He may make known his will to be buried elsewhere. But when the burial takes place within the cathedral, the grave must not be raised. It must be even with the floor and at least 3 1/3 feet (1 meter) removed from the altar.[45] Finally, it is wise to look to the requirements of the civil law in this matter, for in many countries burial within the precincts of a church or of any other building is ruled out as illegal.[46]

---

[40] "Nullus mortuus infra ecclesiam sepeliatur nisi episcopi aut abbates aut digni presbiteres vel fideles laici."—Mansi, XIV, 75.

[41] C. 18, C. XIII, q. II.

[42] *Ius Ecclesiasticum Universum,* lib. IV, tit. XXVIII, n. 4.

[43] *Prompta Bibliotheca,* s.v. "sepultura," n. 5.

[44] Coronata, *De Locis et Temporibus Sacris,* n. 138; Cappello, *Summa,* II, 457; Vermeersch-Creusen, *Epitome,* II, n. 514.

[45] Canon 1202, § 2; Many, *De Locis Sacris,* n. 174; Bouscaren-Ellis, *Canon Law,* p. 603.

[46] Cappello, *Summa,* II, n. 457; Augustine, *Commentary,* VI, 105, 106.

CONCLUSIONS

As a result of this work the following conclusions are offered:

1. Residential Bishops, when they are not under obligation of offering the Holy Sacrifice of the Mass in their cathedrals on Christmas Day, may on that day make use of the privilege which allows them to celebrate successively from midnight the three Masses of the Christmas Liturgy.[1]

2. Bishops may use their portable altar privilege in a bedroom.[2]

3. Bishops enjoy no privilege of reserving the Blessed Sacrament in their chapels, and may reserve the Blessed Sacrament therein only in the circumstances in which the general law allows it.[3]

4. The reservation of the criminal cases of all Bishops to the competence of the Roman Pontiff, as also the reservation of the contentious cases of residential Bishops to the competence of the Sacred Roman Rota, is in force when the Bishop is the defendant, but not when the Bishop is the plaintiff.[4]

5. All Bishops, residential and titular, when they consecrate a church or an altar may, in virtue of the increased faculty granted by Pope Pius XII, grant an indulgence of 100 days to be gained on the anniversary day of the consecration.[5]

6. Bishops and the members of their households may gain by means of a visit to the Bishop's chapel all local indulgences, even though a visit to a specific church in the locality is enjoined as a condition for the gaining of the indulgence.[6]

7. The Bishop's privilege of preaching the word of God everywhere with the presumed consent of the local Ordinary is to be interpreted as the permission to preach everywhere except in those places in which the Bishop is certain that he would be refused permission to preach if such permission were sought.[7]

---

[1] Cf. *supra*, pp. 12, 13.

[2] Cf. *supra*, p. 21.

[3] Cf. *supra*, p. 35.

[4] Cf. *supra*, pp. 46, 55, 56, 101.

[5] Cf. *supra*, pp. 80, 81.

[6] Cf. *supra*, p. 84.

[7] Cf. *supra*, p. 93.

8. Titular Bishops as well as residential Bishops enjoy the privilege of selecting the place in which they will testify when cited in ecclesiastical courts as witnesses.[8]

9. Residential Bishops, by privilege, may take precedence in their own dioceses over both Latin and Oriental Patriarchs and Primates except when the Patriarch or Primate happens to be the residential Bishop's Metropolitan.[9]

10. A residential Bishop who rules two dioceses may impart the papal blessing with the attached plenary indulgence in both dioceses on Easter Sunday, provided that it is physically possible for him to assist at Mass that day in each of the two dioceses.[10]

---

[8] Cf. *supra*, p. 58.

[9] Cf. *supra*, p. 124.

[10] Cf. *supra*, p. 115.

BIBLIOGRAPHY

Sources

Acta Apostolicae Sedis Commentarium Officiale, Romae, 1909-

Acta Sanctae Sedis, 41 vols., Romae, 1865-1908.

Bouscaren, T. Lincoln, *The Canon Law Digest,* 2 vols., Milwaukee: Bruce, 1934, 1943.

Bruns, Hermann T., *Canones Apostolorum et Conciliorum Saeculorum IV-VII,* 2 vols., Berolini, Reimeri, 1839.

Bullarum Diplomatum et Privilegiorum Sanctorum Pontificum Taurinensis Editio, 24 vols. in 25, Augustae Taurinorum, 1857-1872.

Bullarium Franciscanorum, I, Romae, 1759-

Bullarium Ordinis Praedicatorum, I, Romae, 1729-

Caeremoniale Episcoporum Clementis VIII, Innocentii X et Benedicti XIII, iussu editum Benedicti XIV et Leonis XIII, auctoritate recognitum, Ed. Typica, New York: F. Pustet & Co., 1886.

Codex Iuris Canonici Pii X Pontificis Maximi iussu digestus Benedicti Papae XV auctoritate promulgatus, Romae: Typis Polyglottis Vaticanis, 1917.

Codex Theodosianus, ed. Paulus Krueger, Berolini: apud Weidmannos, 1928.

Codicis Iuris Canonici Fontes cura Emi Petri Card. Gasparri editi, 9 vols., Romae (postea Civitate Vaticana): Typis Polyglottis Vaticanis, 1923-1939. (Vols. VII, VIII, IX ed. cura et studio Emi Iustiniani Card. Serédi).

Collectanea S. Congregationis de Propaganda Fide, 2 vols., Romae: Typographia Polyglottis, S.C. de Propaganda Fide, 1907-

Corpus Iuris Canonici, editio Lipsiensis secunda, post Aemilii Richeri curas instruxit Aemilius Friedberg, 2 vols., Lipsiae, 1879-1881.

Corpus Iuris Civilis, Vol. III, Novellae, 5. ed. recognovit Rudolfus Schoell, absolvit Gulielmus Kroll, Berolini: apud Weidmannos, 1928.

Corpus Scriptorum Ecclesiasticorum Latinorum, editum consilio et impensis Academiae Litterarum Caesariae Vindobonensis (*Corpus Vindobonense*), Vindobonae, 1866-

Decreta Authentica Congregationis Sacrorum Rituum, 5 vols., Romae: ex Typographia Polyglotta, 1898-1901. Appendix I, 1912; Appendix II, 1927.

Decreta Authentica Sacrae Congregationis Indulgentiis Sacrisque Reliquiis Praepositae, Ratisbonae, 1883.

Hardouin, Jean, *Acta Conciliorum et Epistolae Decretales ac Constitutiones Summorum Pontificum,* 12 vols., Parisiis, 1714-1715.

Jaffé, Philippus, *Regesta Pontificum Romanorum ab condita Ecclesia ad annum post Christum natum MCXCVIII,* 2. ed. correctam et auctam auspiciis Gulielmi Wattenbach, curaverunt S. Loewenfeld, F. Kaltenbrunner, P. Ewald, 2 vols. in 1, Lipsiae, 1885-1888.

Mansi, Joannes, *Sacrorum Conciliorum Nova et Amplissima Collectio,* 53 vols. in 60, Parisiis, 1901-1927.

Missale Romanum ex decreto Sacrosancti Concilii Tridentini restitutum S. Pii. V Pontificis Maximi iussu editum aliorum pontificum cura recognitum a Pio X reformatum et Benedicti XV auctoritate vulgatum, editio XIV iuxta Typicam Vaticanam, Ratisbonae: Sumptibus et Typis F. Pustet, 1930.

Pontificale Romanum Summorum Pontificum iussu editum a Benedicto XIV et Leone XIII Pont. Max. recognitum et castigatum, ed. secunda, New York: F. Pustet, 1908.

Preces et Pia Opera in Favorem Omnium Christifidelium Vel Quorumdam Coetuum Personarum Indulgentiis Ditata et Opportune Recognita, Civitate Vaticana: Typis Polyglottis Vaticanis, 1938.

Potthast, Augustus, *Regesta Pontificum Romanorum inde ab A. post Christum natum 1198 ad A. 1304,* 2 vols., Berolini, 1874-1875.

Rituale Romanum Pauli V Pontificis Maximi iussu editum aliorumque Pontificum cura recognitum atque auctoritate SSmi D.M. Pii Papae XI ad normam Codicis Iuris Canonici accomodatum, 2. ed., *iuxta Typicam,* Ratisbonae: F. Pustet, 1929.

Sacrae Romanae Rotae Decisiones seu Sententiae (ab anno 1909-), Romae: Typis Vaticanis, 1912-

Schroeder, H. J., *Canons and Decrees of the Council of Trent,* St. Louis: B. Herder Book Co., 1941.

Reference Works

Attwater, Donald, *A Catholic Dictionary,* New York: Macmillan Co., 1941.

Augustine, Charles, *A Commentary on the New Code of Canon Law,* 8 vols., St. Louis: B. Herder Book Co.: Vol. I, 1918; Vols. II, III, V, 1919; Vol. IV, 1920; Vol. VI, 1921; Vol. VII, 1923; Vol. VIII, 1922.

———, *Liturgical Law,* A Handbook of the Roman Liturgy, St. Louis and London: B. Herder Book Co., 1931.

———, *Rights and Duties of Ordinaries,* St. Louis: B. Herder Book Co., 1924.

Ayrinhac, H. A.; *Administrative Legislation in the New Code of Canon Law,* New York: Longmans, Green & Co., 1930.

———, *Penal Legislation in the New Code of Canon Law,* revised by P. J. Lydon, New York: Benziger, 1936.

Bachofen, A., *Summa Iuris Ecclesiastici Publici,* New York: F. Pustet, 1910.

Badii, C., *Institutiones Iuris Canonici,* 2 vols., Florentiae, Vol. I, 3. ed., 1921; Vol. II, 3. ed., 1922.

Barbosa, A., *Iuris ecclesiastici universi libri III,* 3 vols., Lugduni, 1650.

———, *Pastoralis Sollicitudinis sive de Officio et Potestate Episcopi Tripartita Descriptio,* Lugduni, 1656.

Benedictus XIV, *De Synodo Dioecesana,* 2. Parmensis ed., 2 vols., 1764.

Beringer, F., *Les Indulgences Leur Nature et Leur Usage,* 3. ed., Traduction par L'Abbé Ph. Mazoyer, 2 vols., Paris: P. Lethielleux, 1905.

Berutti, C., *Institutiones Iuris Canonici,* 6 vols., Vol. II, Pars I, 1943; Vol. VI, 1938; Taurini-Romae: Marietti.

Beste, U., *Introductio in Codicem,* 2. ed., Collegeville, Minn.: St. John's Abbey Press, 1944.

Bevilacqua, A., *De Episcopi seu Ordinarii ex Nova Codice Canonico Iuribus ac Obligationibus,* New York: F. Pustet, 1921.

Blat, A., *Commentarium Textus Codicis Iuris Canonici,* 5 vols, in 7, Romae: apud Angelicum, 1921-1927. Lib. I, 1921; Lib. II, 2. ed., 1921; Lib. III, pars I, 2. ed., 1924; lib. III, partes II-VI, 1923; Lib. IV, 1927; Lib. V, 1924.

Bliley, Nicholas, *Altars according to the Code of Canon Law,* The Catholic University of America Canon Law Studies, n. 38, Washington, D. C.: The Catholic University of America, 1927.

Bollandus, J., *Acta Sanctorum,* Martii Tomus Tertius, Parisiis et Romae: apud Victorem Palmé Bibliopolam, 1865.

Bouix, D., *Tractatus de Episcopo,* 2 vols., Parisiis, 1873.

Bouscaren, T. Lincoln-Ellis, Adam C., *Canon Law, Text and Commentary,* Milwaukee: Bruce Publishing Co., 1946.

Bouuaert, F. Claeys-Simenon, G., *Manuale Juris Canonici,* 3 vols., Vols. I et III, 3. ed., Vol. II, 1. ed., Gandae et Leodii: H. Dessain, 1930-1931.

Burke, Thomas, *Competence in Ecclesiastical Tribunals,* The Catholic University of America Canon Law Studies, n. 14, Washington, D. C.: The Catholic University of America, 1922.

Callewaert, C., *Liturgicae Institutiones, Tractatus Primus de S. Liturgia Universim,* 2. ed., Brugis: apud Carolum Beyaert, Editorem Pontificium, 1925.

Cance, Adrien, *Le Code de Droit canonique,* 3. ed., 3 vols., Paris: Lecoffre, 1933-1934.

Cappello, Felix, *De Curia Romana iuxta Reformationem a Pio X,* Vol. I, *De Curia Romana, "Sede Plena,"* Romae: F. Pustet, 1911.

——, *Summa Iuris Canonici,* 3 vols., Romae: apud Aedes Universitatis Gregorianae, 1940-1945. Vols. I et II, 4. ed., 1945; Vol. III, 2. ed., 1940.

——, *Tractatus Canonico-Moralis de Censuris,* Taurinorum Augustae: Marietti, 1925.

——, *Tractatus Canonico-Moralis de Sacramentis iuxta Codicem Iuris Canonici,* 5 vols., Romae: Marietti, 1942-1947. Vol. I, 4. ed., 1945; Vol. II, 4. ed., 1944; Vol. III, 2. ed., 1942; Vol. IV, editio altera accurate recognita et aucta, 1947; Vol. V, 5. ed., 1947.

Catalanus, Joseph, *Caeremoniale Episcoporum in Duos Libros Distributum Clementis VIII et Innocentii X nunc Primum Commentariis Illustratum,* Paris: Sumptibus A. Jouby, 1860.

———, *Pontificale Romanum in Tres Partes Distributum Clementis VIII ac Urbani VIII Auctoritate, nunc primum Prolegomenis et Commentariis Ilustratum,* 3 vols., Paris: Sumptibus J. Leroux et Jouby, 1852.

Chelodi, Ioannes, *Ius de Personis,* 2. ed., a sac. Ernesto Bertagnolli, Tridenti: Libr. edit. Tridentum, 1927.

———, *Ius Poenale et Ordo Procedendi in Iudiciis Criminalibus iuxta Codicem Iuris Canonici,* Tridenti: Libr. edit. Tridentum, 1925 [1920].

Cicognani, Amleto, *Canon Law,* 2. revised ed., authorized English version by J. O'Hara and F. Brennan, Westminster: Newman Bookshop, 1946.

Cocchi, Guidus, *Commentarium in Codicem Iuris Canonici,* 8 vols. in 5, Taurini-Romae: Marietti, Vol. V, 4. ed., 1942.

Coronata, Matthaeus Conte a, *De Locis et Temporibus Sacris,* Augustae Taurinorum: Marietti, 1922.

———, *Institutiones Iuris Canonici ad Usum Utriusque Cleri et Scholarum,* 5 vols., Romae: Marietti, 1936-1945. Vols. I et II, 2. ed., 1939; Vol. III, 2. ed., 1941; Vol. IV, 2. ed., 1945; Vol. V, 1936.

———, *Institutiones Iuris Canonici ad Usum Utriusque Cleri et Scholarum, de Sacramentis, Tractatus Canonicus,* 3 vols., Romae: Marietti, 1943-1946. Vol. I, 1943; Vol. II, 1945; Vol. III, 1946.

Davis, Henry, *Moral and Pastoral Theology,* 4 vols., 4. ed., New York: Sheed and Ward, 1943.

De Angelis, Philippus, *Praelectiones Iuris Canonici,* 3 vols., Romae: Desclée, 1908.

De Angelis, Seraphinus, *De Indulgentiis, Tractatus Quoad Earum Naturam et Usum,* Colle Don Bosco [Asti]: Libreria Dottrina Cristiana, 1946.

De Herdt, J. B., *Praxis Pontificalis seu Caeremonialis Episcoporum Practica Expositio,* 2. ed., 3 vols., Lovanii, 1906.

De Meester, A., *Juris Canonici et Juris Canonico-Civilis Compendium,* nova editio, 3 vols. in 4, Brugis: Desclée, 1921-1928. Vol. I, 1921; Vol. II, 1923; Vol. III, Pars I, 1926; Vol. III, Pars II, 1928.

Devoti, I., *Ius Canonicum Universum Publicum et Privatum,* 3 vols., Romae, 1837.

Downs, John E., *The Concept of Clerical Immunity,* The Catholic University of America Canon Law Studies, n. 126, Washington, D. C.: The Catholic University of America Press, 1941.

Durandus, G., *Rationale Divinorum Officiorum,* accedit aliud Divinorum Officiorum Rationale a Joanne Belethro, Napoli, 1895.

Fagnanus, Prosper, *Commentaria in Quinque Libros Decretalium,* 5 vols. in 3, Venetiis, 1696.

Fanfani, Ludovicus, *De Indulgentiis, Manuale Theoretico-Practicum ad Normam Codicis Iuris Canonici,* 2. ed., notabiliter aucta, Taurini-Romae: Marietti, 1926.

Ferraris, Lucius, *Prompta Bibliotheca Canonica, Iuridica Moralis, Theologica, necnon Ascetica, Polemica, Rubricistica, Historica,* 9 vols., Romae, 1885-1899.

Gasparri, Petrus, *Tractatus Canonicus de Sanctissima Eucharistia,* 2 vols., Parisiis et Lugduni, 1897.

Gattico, J., *De Oratoriis Domesticis et de Usu Altaris Portatilis,* Romae, 1747.

Goyeneche, S., *De Processibus Breves Adnotationes ad L. IV Codicis Iuris Canonici, Vol. I, De Iudiciis in Genere,* pro manuscripto, Romae: ad S. Ioannis Lat.

Hagedorn, Francis, *General Legislation on Indulgences,* The Catholic University of America Canon Law Studies, n. 22, Washington, D. C.: The Catholic University of America, 1924.

Hynes, Harry, *The Privileges of Cardinals,* The Catholic University of America Canon Law Studies, n. 217, Washington, D. C.: The Catholic University of America Press, 1945.

Kelly, James, *The Jurisdiction of the Confessor according to the Code of Canon Law,* New York: Benziger, 1928.

Lega, M. Card., *Praelectiones in Textum Iuris Canonici, de Delictis et Poenis,* 2. ed., Romae, 1910.

———, *Praelectionis in Textum Iuris Canonici, de Iudiciis Ecclesiasticis,* 2 lib. in 4 vols., Romae, 1896-1901.

———, -Bartoccetti, V., *Commentarius in Iudicia Ecclesiastica iuxta Codicem Iuris Canonici,* 3 vols., Vol. I, 1938; Vol. II, 1939; Vol. III, 1941; Romae: Anonima Libraria Cattolica Italiana.

Lepicier, Card. Alexis, *Indulgences, Their Origin, Nature and Development,* 3. English ed., London: Burns, Oates & Washbourne, Ltd., 1928.

Lynch, George, *Coadjutors and Auxiliaries of Bishops,* The Catholic University of America Canon Law Studies, n. 238, Washington, D. C.: The Catholic University of America Press, 1947.

Many, S., *Praelectiones Canonicae de Locis Sacris,* Parisiis, 1904.

Maroto, P., *Institutiones Iuris Canonici ad Normam Novi Codicis,* 2 vols., Vol. I, 3. ed., 1921; Vol. II, 1919, Romae: Apud Commentarium pro Religiosis.

McDonough, Thomas, *Apostolic Administrators,* The Catholic University of America Canon Law Studies, n. 139, Washington, D. C.: The Catholic University of America Press, 1941.

McSorley, *An Outline History of the Church by Centuries,* St. Louis: B. Herder Book Co., 1944.

Michiels, G., *Principia Generalia de Personis in Ecclesia, Commentarius Libri II Codicis Canonici, Canones Praeliminares* (87-106), Belgium: Brasschaat, 1932.

Migne, J. P., *Patrologiae Cursus Completus, Series Graeca,* 161 vols., Parisiis, 1856-1866.

———, *Patrologiae Cursus Completus, Series Latina,* 221 vols.., Parisiis, 1844-1864.

Monin, Arthur, *De Curia Romana: Eius Historia ac Hodierna Disciplina iuxta Reformationem a Pio X Inductam,* Lovanii, 1912.

Moretti, Aloisius, *Caeremoniale iuxta Ritum Romanum seu de Sacris Functionibus, Episcopo Celebrante-Assistente-Absente,* 4 vols., Taurini: Marietti, Vol. I, 1936; Vol. II, 1937; Vol. III, 1938; Vol. IV, 1939.

Morinus, J., *Commentarius Historicus de Disciplina in Administratione Sacramenti Poenitentiae, lib. IX,* Venetiis, 1702.

Mourret, F., *A History of the Catholic Church,* 6 vols., St. Louis: B. Herder Book Co., 1946-1947, translated by N. Thompson.

Nabuco, J., *Pontificalis Romani Expositio Juridico-Practica,* 3 vols., Petropoli-Brasilia: Sumptibus Editõria Vozes, LTDA., 1945.

Nainfa, John, *Costume of Prelates of the Catholic Church,* new and revised ed., Baltimore: John Murphy Co., 1926.

Noval, J., *Commentarium Codicis Iuris Canonici,* Lib. IV, *De Processibus,* Pars I, *De Iudiciis,* Augustae Taurinorum: Marietti, 1920.

O'Connell, J., *The Celebration of Mass,* 3 vols., Milwaukee: Bruce Publishing Co., 1940-1941.

Paschang, J., *The Sacramentals according to the Code of Canon Law,* The Catholic University of America Canon Law Studies, n. 28, Washington, D. C.: The Catholic University of America, 1925.

Pernicone, J., *The Ecclesiastical Prohibition of Books,* The Catholic University of America Canon Law Studies, n. 72, Washington, D. C.: The Catholic University of America, 1932.

Petra, Vincentius, Card., *Commentaria ad Constitutiones Apostolicas,* 5 tom. in 2 vols., Venetiis, 1729.

Raus, J. B., *Institutiones Canonicae iuxta Novum Codicem Juris Pro Scholis vel ad Usum Privatum Synthetice Redactae,* 2. ed., Parisiis: Typis Emmanuelis Vitte, 1931.

Regatillo, E., *Institutiones Iuris Canonici,* 2 vols., Vol. I, 1941; Vol. II, 1942, Santander: Sal Terrae.

———, *Ius Sacramentarium,* 2 vols., Vol. I, 1945; Vol. II, 1946, Santander: Sal Terrae.

Reiffenstuel, Anacletus, *Ius Canonicum Universum,* 5 vols. in 6, Romae, 1831-1834.

Roberti, F., *Codicis Iuris Canonici Schemata,* Lib. IV, *De Processibus,* I, *De Iudiciis in Genere,* in Civitate Vaticana: Typis Polyglottis Vaticanis, 1940.

———, *De Processibus,* 2 vols., Vol. I, 2. ed., 1941; Vol. II, 1927, Romae: Apud Custodiam Librariam Pontificii Instituti Utriusque Iuris.

Roelker, E., *Principles of Privilege according to the Code of Canon Law,* The Catholic University of America Canon Law Studies, n. 35, Washington, D. C.: The Catholic University of America, 1926.

Santi, F., *Praelectiones Iuris Canonici iuxta Ordinem Decretalium Gregorii IX,* 5 vols. in 2, New York, 1886.

Schmalzgrueber, F., *Ius Ecclesiasticum Universum,* 5 vols. in 12, Romae, 1843-1845.

Schroeder, H. J., *Disciplinary Decrees of the General Councils,* Text, Translation and Commentary, St. Louis and London: B. Herder Book Co., 1937.

Schulte, A. J., *Benedicenda,* New York: Benziger, 1907.

Sipos, S., *Enchiridion Iuris Canonici,* 2. ed., Pécs, Hungary: Haladás, R.T., 1931.

Sleutjes, M., *Instructio de Stationibus S. Viae Crucis,* 5. ed. recognita a Fr. Bertrando Kurtschied, ad Claras Aquas: ex Typographia Collegii S. Bonaventurae, 1927.

Smith, S. B., *Elements of Ecclesiastical Law Adapted especially to the Discipline of the Church in the United States,* 3 vols., Vol. I, *Ecclesiastical Persons,* 9. ed., New York: Benziger, 1887.

Sole, J., *Praelectiones in Lib. V Codicis Iuris Canonici, De Delictis et Poenis,* Romae: Pustet, 1920.

Solieri, F., *Institutiones Iuris Ecclesiastici,* 2. ed., Romae: Pustet, 1921.

Thomassinus, L., *Vetus et Nova Ecclesiae Disciplina circa Beneficia et Beneficiarios,* 3 tom. in 10 vols., Magontiaci, 1787.

Toso, Albertus, *Ad Codicem Iuris Canonici Commentaria Minora,* 5 vols., Vol. II, tom. I, 1922; Vol. II, tom. II, 1923, Romae: Marietti.

Vacandard, E., *The Inquisition,* translated from 2. French ed., by Bertrand L. Conway, New York: Longmans, Green & Co., 1915.

Van Hove, A., *Commentarium Lovaniense in Codicem Iuris Canonici,* Vol. I, tom. I, *Prolegomena ad Codicem Iuris Canonici,* 2. ed., Mechliniae et Romae: Dessain, 1945; Vol. I, tom. III, *De Consuetudine, De Temporis Supputatione,* Mechliniae et Romae: Dessain, 1933; Vol. I, tom. V, *De Privilegiis, de Dispensationibus,* Mechliniae et Romae: Dessain, 1939.

Vermeersch A.-Creusen, J., *Epitome Iuris Canonici,* 3 vols., Mechliniae et Romae: H. Dessain, Vol. I, 6. ed., 1937; Vol. II, 6. ed., 1940; Vol. III, 6. ed., 1946.

Vives, Joseph C., Card., *De Dignitate et Officiis Episcoporum et Praelatorum Tractatus Canonico—Moralis,* Romae: Pustet, 1895.

Wernz, F., *Ius Decretalium,* 2. ed., 6 vols. in 10, Romae et Prati, 1906-1913.

———, -Vidal, P., *Ius Canonicum,* 7 vols. in 9, Romae: Universitas Gregoriana, 1927-1946. Vol. I, 1938; Vol. II, 3. ed., a P. Philippo Aguirre recognita, 1943; Vol. III, 1933; Vol. IV, Pars I, 1934; Vol. IV, Pars II, 1935; Vol. V, 3. ed., a P. Philippo Aguirre recognita, 1946; Vol. VI, Pars I, 1927; Vol. VI, Pars II, 1928; Vol. VII, 1937.

Woywod, S., *A Practical Commentary on the Code of Canon Law,* 2 vols., 10th printing, revised by Callistus Smith, New York: Joseph F. Wagner, 1946.

Wuest, J., *Matters Liturgical,* translated and revised by Thos. Mullaney, New York: Pustet, 6. ed., 1944.

ARTICLES

Ayrinhac, H. A., "The Motu Proprio '*Quantavis Diligentia*'"—*The Ecclesiastical Review*, XLVII (1912), 303-316.

Berutti, C., "De Iurisdictione Quae Ipso Facto Iure Delegatur ad Audiendas Fidelium Confessiones"—*Jus Pontificium*, XIV (1934), 51-66; 216-220.

Hannan, J., "Cases and Studies"—*The Jurist*, VIII (1948), 70, 71.

Larraona, "Adnotationes"—*Commentarium pro Religiosis*, XII (1931), 11-12.

Maroto, P., "De Sacris Benedictionibus"—*Apollinaris*, II (1929), 243-245.

———, "Adimadversiones ad Secundum Responsum PCI die 29 maii 1934"—*Apollinaris*, VIII (1935), 51-54.

Melata, B., "An Missa et Indulgentia Altaris Privilegiati Reparari Possint"—*Analecta Ecclesiastica*, III (1895), 83-86.

———, "De Benedictione Papale Eiusque Ritu Servando"—*Analecta Ecclesiastica*, III (1895), 36-41.

Mutch, F. J., "Apostolic Indulgences and the Rosary"—*The Homiletic and Pastoral Review*, XLIII (1942-1943), 429-436.

———, "Episcopal Indulgences"—*The Homiletic and Pastoral Review*, XLVII (1947), 216, 217.

Roberti, F., "De Foro Competenti"—*Apollinaris*, III (1930), 145-146.

Schroeder, F. J., "The Church and the Abuse of Indulgences in the Middle Ages"—*American Catholic Quarterly Review*, XLV (1921), 178-205.

Teodori, I., "Privilegium Canonis—Consultationes"—*Apollinaris*, V (1932), 112-116.

Vermeersch, A., "Consultationes"—*Periodica*, X (1922), 95.

———, "De Locis in Quibus Episcopi Indulgentias Concedere Possunt"—*Periodica*, XIX (1930), 25*, 26*.

Woywod, S., "Procedural Law of the Church"—*The Homiletic and Pastoral Review*, XXX (1930), 725-732.

PERIODICALS

American Catholic Quarterly Review, Philadelphia, 1876-1924.

American Ecclesiastical Review, The, Vols. I-XXXII, Philadelphia, 1895-1905; from 1905: *The Ecclesiastical Review*, Vols. XXXIII-CIX, Philadelphia, 1905-1943; from 1944: The American Ecclesiastical Review, Washington, D. C., Vol. CX- , 1944-

Analecta Ecclesiastica, Romae, 1893-1911.

Apollinaris, Romae, 1928-

Commentarium pro Religiosis, Romae, 1920; ab anno 1935: *Commentarium pro Religiosis et Missionariis.*

Homiletic and Pastoral Review, The, New York, 1900-

Jurist, The, Washington, D. C.: The Catholic University of America, 1941-

Jus Pontificium, Romae, 1921-1940.

Periodica de Religiosis et Missionariis, Brugis, 1905-1919; *Periodica de Re Canonica et Morali utili praesertim Religiosis et Missionariis*, 1920-1927; *Periodica de Re Canonica, Morali, Liturgica*, 1927-

ABBREVIATIONS

AAS—*Acta Apostolicae Sedis.*

AER—*The American Ecclesiastical Review.*

ASS—*Acta Sanctae Sedis.*

Bull. Rom.—*Bullarum Diplomatum et Privilegiorum Sanctorum Pontificum Taurinensis Editio.*

Decr. Auth.—*Decreta Authentica Congregationis Sacrorum Rituum.*

Decr. Auth. S.C. Indulg.—*Decreta Authentica Sacrae Congregationis Indulgentiis Sacrisque Reliquiis Praepositae.*

ER—*The Ecclesiastical Review.*

Fontes—*Codicis Iuris Canonici Fontes cura . . . Gasparri editi.*

MPG—Migne, *Patrologia Graeca.*

MPL—Migne, *Patrologia Latina.*

PCI—Pontificia Commissio ad Codicis Canones authentice Interpretandos.

S.C.C.—Sacra Congregatio Concilii.

S.C. Indulg.—Sacra Congregatio Indulgentiis Sacrisque Reliquiis Praeposita.

S.C. de Prop. Fide—Sacra Congregatio de Propaganda Fide.

S.C.S. Off.—Suprema Congregatio Sancti Officii.

S.R.C.—Sacrorum Rituum Congregatio.

BIOGRAPHICAL NOTE

Francis J. McElroy was born August 11, 1917, in Philadelphia, Pennsylvania. He attended the Academy of Mercy and St. Joseph's Preparatory School in that city. In September of 1935 he enrolled at St. Joseph's College from which he received the Bachelor of Arts degree in 1939. In the same year he was admitted to the Seminary of St. Charles Borromeo, where he completed his course in Philosophy and Theology. He was ordained to the Sacred Priesthood on February 24, 1945. In the fall of that year he enrolled in the School of Canon Law of the Catholic University of America, where he received the degree of the Baccalaureate in Canon Law in June of 1946, and the degree of the Licentiate in Canon Law in June of 1947.

ALPHABETICAL INDEX

CANON LAW STUDIES*

306. WATERS, REV. JOSEPH L., S.S.J., J.C.L., The Probation in Societies of Quasi-Religious.
307. REGAN, REV. MICHAEL J., J.C.L., Canon 16.
308. BYRNE, REV. HARRY J., J.C.L., Investment of Church Funds.
309. GALLAGHER, REV. THOMAS V., J.C.L., The Rejection of Judicial Witnesses and Testimony.
310. CHATHAM, REV. JOSIAH G., Ph.D., S.T.L., J.C.L., Force and Fear as Invalidating Marriage: The Element of Injustice.
311. BROWN, REV. JAMES VICTOR, O.R.S.A., J.C.L., The Invalidating Effects of Force, Fear, and Fraud upon the Canonical Novitiate.
312. DUERR, REV. CHARLES J., B.A., J.C.L., The Judicial Notary.
313. GONZALEZ, REV. FRANCISCO J., O.S.A., J.C.L., De Parocho Religioso Eiusque Superiore Locali.
314. HANNON, REV. JAMES J., J.C.L., Holy Viaticum.
315. SADLOWSKI, REV. ERWIN L., J.C.L., The Sacred Furnishings of Churches.
316. SEGO, REV. ARTHUR A., J.C.L., Dispensation from the Interpellations.
317. WATERHOUSE, REV. JOHN M., J.C.L., The Power of the Local Ordinary to Impose a Matrimonial Ban.
318. FREIN, REV. EUGENE B., J.C.L., The Discretionary Power of the Defender of the Matrimonial Bond.
319. CARTON, REV. GEORGE A., J.C.L., The Time Factor in the Gaining of Indulgences.
320. WALSH, REV. JOHN J., C.C.Sp., J.C.L., The Jurisdiction of the Inter-ritual Confessor in the United States and Canada.
321. UNTERKOEFLER, REV. ERNST L., S.T.L., J.C.L., The Presiding Judge in Matrimonial Causes of First Instance.

---

*A complete list of the available numbers in the series will be found in earlier studies. Send orders to The Catholic University of America Press, 620 Michigan Avenue, N.E., Washington 17, D. C.

www.ingramcontent.com/pod-product-compliance
Lightning Source LLC
LaVergne TN
LVHW050217080826
844660LV00012B/423

* 9 7 8 0 8 1 3 2 2 4 5 8 9 *